$\mathcal{W}$ILDERNESS WANDERINGS
A LENTEN PILGRIMAGE

MARILYN BROWN ODEN

Scripture quotations not otherwise identified are from the New Revised Standard Version of the Bible, copyright 1989 by the Division of Christian Education of the National Council of the Churches of Christ in the USA and are used by permission.

Scripture quotations designated RSV are from the Revised Standard Version of the Bible, copyrighted 1946, 1952, and © 1971 by the Division of Christian Education, National Council of the Churches of Christ in the USA. Used by permission.

Scripture quotations designated NEB are from *The New English Bible.* © The Delegates of Oxford University Press and The Syndics of the Cambridge University Press 1961, 1970. Reprinted with permission.

The adaptation of an African model for Bible study is from the Lumko Missiological Institute of South Africa. From The Pastoral Use of the Bible, Lumko Institute, Germiston, 1991. Used with permission of the Lumko Institute.

Cover design: Jim Bateman
First Printing: November 1995 (7)
ISBN: 0-8358-0743-6
Library of Congress Catalog Card Number: 95-60924
Printed in the United States of America

WILDERNESS WANDERINGS

A LENTEN PILGRIMAGE

To Danna Lee, Dirk, Valerie, Bryant,

Angela, and Mark

Contents

◇

Acknowledgments

✧

I WANT TO EXPRESS APPRECIATION of my husband Bill for his excellent help as a theologian and also as a critic—and for his honoring my time in "study hall" while I wrote *Wilderness Wanderings*. I am grateful also to Carolyn Waters, a United Methodist clergywoman who serves as a district superintendent in the Nebraska Conference, for her reading and critique of the manuscript. Her insight and suggestions were most helpful. Dozens of people walked with me through this Lenten pilgrimage, some on the pages of this book, others in my heart; some nearby, others far away; some living now, others who've gone before. I am thankful for the touch of each one; they all helped me hold the pen as the words came.

Introduction

—————————————————————————— ✧

The purpose of *Wilderness Wanderings* is to help us prepare for Easter through the use of scripture, readings, guided reflections, and prayer aimed toward the examination of our spiritual journey in the shadow of the cross and toward the awakening of our hearts and minds to the opportunity for new life offered by our Easter faith.

The chapters correspond with the weeks of Lent: chapter 1 for the first week of Lent, chapter 2 for the second week, and so on, with chapter 6 being read during Holy Week. Chapter 7 is for Easter morning. The forty scripture readings begin with FAITH AND TRANSFORMATION in chapter 1. A scripture reading accompanies each meditation throughout the rest of the book. Chapters 2 through 6 have seven meditations to facilitate daily reading. The book is a resource for an individual pilgrimage through Lent, a group pilgrimage, or a Lenten retreat. *Wilderness Wanderings* includes a guide at the end of the book.

If *Wanderers* choose a group pilgrimage, consider forming special Lenten groups. I recommend that the groups consist of eight to ten people who come together for seven sessions, beginning Ash Wednesday. However, the *Wanderers* may make the pilgrimage in six sessions if a congregation chooses to begin Lenten groups the first week of Lent or if a church school class uses this material for a Lenten series. For these sessions, I would suggest that large church school classes form groups of eight to ten persons, with the same people in each group each week.

Now let us venture forth as wilderness wanderers on a Lenten pilgrimage of self-examination and spiritual renewal.

1

Wandering in the Wilderness

✧

Our first family backpacking trip began in the dim light of dawn with God's small creatures singing their sunrise songs. My husband Bill, our four children, and I stepped into the San Juan wilderness of the Colorado Rockies with compass and topographical map in hand. Even our youngest, four years old, carried a day pack filled with socks.

We wound our way upward through the spruce-scented forests and colorful mountain meadows, over loose shale and craggy rocks. Finally, late that afternoon we reached a clear blue lake near the summit of Table Mountain. Feeling weary and heavy laden, we set up camp. We tied a rope between two spruce trees, draped a large plastic tarp over the rope, secured it with clothespins, and called it a tent. We built a fire, carried water from the lake, and ate freeze-dried manna (definitely not from heaven). A bit smug about being an adventurous family, we moleskinned our blisters, treed our packs—and accidentally smashed our compass! GOD THING?

The next morning we set out again, undaunted (but less smug). As the morning wore on, we realized we were lost. Stooped with the weight of our packs and unsure of our direction, we longed for the place we'd left behind. We struggled up ravines and stumbled down rock slides, balanced on logs to cross rushing streams and fought our way through scratchy willows higher than everyone's head but Bill's. No compass. No trail. No landmarks that were shown on the topog map.

I desperately wanted to see an initialed tree, a rusty can, a bit of litter—any sign that others had passed here before. Nothing. Not so much as a gum wrapper.

If only we had a compass!

WE ARE THE *LAOS*, the people of God, called to be the church. But sometimes we feel lost—as persons and as communities of faith. We stoop with the weight of our burdens, unsure of our direction, longing for a simpler day. We struggle with new challenges and stumble over old obstacles. We balance precariously, trying to bridge the chasms in today's world, and at times we feel we are hopelessly in over our heads.

In this new day, we still feel the age-old spiritual void. We know in our hearts that the Word and our traditions have filled that void in the past. But our heads aren't sure we can trust these anymore; the terrain has changed since the maps were drawn. Lent offers us a special opportunity to reflect on how we translate that precious Word and those life-giving traditions for our present world, for our own life and our congregational life together. It is a season for spiritual renewal even in this new day.

Let's get off the expressways and out of the crowds and wander into the wilderness to look for the compass. Come! Let's walk the ancient paths of the saints; and when we wander off to pick our own way through today's confusing maze, let's remain within the sound of their voices, listening for them to point the way. Come! Let's read the scriptures and pray, reflect on the meaning of our baptism, review and renew our spiritual pilgrimage, rekindle the flame of discipleship, and rejoice in a new dawn. Come! Let's wander through the wilderness, grateful that we can walk without fear for we are assured that resurrection follows crucifixion, rebirth follows pain, and new life follows death.

FACT AND TRADITION

Recently two of our children, now grown, sat around the dinner table with Bill and me on *Mardi Gras*—a holiday we adopted when we moved to southern Louisiana.

Our daughter asked, "Have you thought of a title for your book about Lent?"

I shook my head. "Not yet."

"What does *Lent* come from?" asked our son, glancing up at me from his apple pie.

"It's derived from *lang*," I said, "meaning 'long,' because the days grow longer in spring."

"That makes sense."

Knowing full well this was answer enough, I still was pulled toward the universal and ineffectual parental tendency to expound—regardless of the age of the children. I stopped stirring my coffee and put the spoon on my saucer. "It's from *lenten* or *lente* in Middle English. And *lencten* or *lengten* in the Anglo-Saxon. It means 'spring.'" *(lengthen ?) –*

I started to tell him that we gain eighty to ninety minutes of daylight between Ash Wednesday and Easter in the northern hemisphere. And that in the southern hemisphere the Lenten season falls in autumn. But he politely stifled a yawn.

"How about *Wilderness Wanderings* for a title?" suggested Bill.

I thought about it for a moment. "I like that. It fits."

Our son stopped concentrating on scooping up the melted ice cream with his fork. "Why *wanderings*?"

"Because Lent invites us to make a pilgrimage," I explained. "And if we're open to the Spirit, it's not a prescheduled trip but an open-ended journey—a process instead of a destination."

"I see that," said our daughter. "But why *wilderness*?"

"Why not?" I asked.

"I thought Jesus went into the wilderness at the beginning of his ministry. Not at the end."

Bill nodded to her. "Right after his baptism. The forty days of Lent are traditionally based on his forty days in the wilderness."

(good explanation)

"Also the Hebrews wandered in the wilderness for forty years with Moses." Risking another stifled yawn, I added, "Another 'forty' is that in the scriptures, Jesus' resurrection appearances extended over forty days."

Our son frowned. "Lent begins tomorrow with Ash Wednesday and includes the next six weeks before Easter?"

"Yes."

With a patient role-reversal look on his face, he put down his fork. "Don't say in your book that Lent has forty days. It has forty-*six* days."

I smiled, appreciating his concern. "The early church didn't count Sundays in the Lenten season."

"That's odd."

"Lent was a time of self-denial, fasting, and penitence. But in the early church fasting was forbidden on Sunday because it was the weekly celebration of the Resurrection."

"So if a guy gave up hot apple pie and ice cream for Lent, he could still have it on Sundays." He grinned, shifting the mood. Enough serious table talk.

AS THE CONVERSATION CHANGED to lighter topics, my mind lingered on Lent and its traditions. Tomorrow would be Ash Wednesday, the day of penitence that originated in early medieval times. In Ash Wednesday services, a cross of ashes on our foreheads would call us to confront our own mortality ("Remember that you are dust, and to dust you shall return") and to confess before God our sins ("Repent, and believe the gospel").[1] Tomorrow we would take our first step into the wilderness and begin the Lenten season of self-examination and spiritual renewal.

I thought about Lent through the ages. Historically Lent was a time for training candidates for baptism. Their instruction spread over a six-week period to help ensure that only those who sincerely professed Christ were received. The six weeks was a time of discipline and renewal for the whole church since the members were expected to reflect upon their own baptismal journey and to renew their baptismal vows.

Lent also became a time of penance for those who had committed grave sins and who had applied for reinstatement into the church. The lamentation for the penitents' sins intensified the somber mood of the Lenten season, sometimes belaboring guilt to the point of morbidity. I remembered reading that Lent was probably the most abused season of the faith journey, becoming at times "a period of excessive introspection, empty abstinence from tidbits of affluence, and the enjoyment of the gloom of self-denial."[2] Lent is indeed a deeply serious season, but it is also a profoundly joyous one. Not only do we confess and repent, but we also remember that God is gracious and loving and does not give up on us. As we journey toward the cross, both as persons and congregations, we do so in full awareness of the Resurrection.

—— ✧ ——

HEARING MY NAME, I brought my thoughts back to the table. After dinner I would clear away the green, purple, and gold glitter of *Mardi Gras*. Tomorrow I would detour from the facades and frivolity of its carnival world with the gaudy parades and tossed tidbits—the world in which everyone lives. Tomorrow all of us in God's family who call ourselves Christians would receive the invitation to unmask and repent, to wander in the wilderness and reach for the sacred.

What does Mardi Gras mean?

FAITH AND TRANSFORMATION

Scripture: Joel 2:1-2, 12-17

As we ponder the meaning of Lent, our heads ask, *Where did it come from?* That is the question of fact and tradition; it looks at the past. But our hearts ask, *What does it mean?* That is the question of faith and transformation; it looks at the present. Moses ventured into the wilderness to lead God's people out of bondage into the promised land, and Jesus ventured into the wilderness to prepare for the ministry ahead and to be faithful in temptation. We venture into the wilderness during this holy season to allow deepened faith to transform us.

Joel clearly states the purpose of our Lenten journey: "Yet even now, says the Lord, return to me with all your heart." The human heart is so important in the Hebrew Scriptures that it refers to the heart 814 times. In those scriptures the heart represents the total person. It is the center of emotions and moods, understanding and wisdom, devotion and conversion. It is the place in which decisions are made, obedience conveyed, and good and evil discerned. The heart is the hub around which the spokes of the wheel of one's life revolve. To return to God with all one's heart is to place God—the One whose love heals and reconciles—at the hub of life, so that all relationships, deeds, and words extend like spokes from that center. Lent is a season for holistic renewal through study and prayer, worship and praise, humility and discipline. It is a time to transform the center of our being and doing.

Our wilderness pilgrimage is paradoxical. In *Here and Now* Henri J. M. Nouwen says that the great paradox of the spiritual life is "that the most personal is most universal, that the most intimate, is most communal, and that the most contemplative is most active." As we walk in the wilderness, we step to the Lenten rhythm with its upbeat of contemplation and its downbeat of action. We are led to the private place of solitude and the corporate place of worship. Our soul sings the solo of the intimate and also joins the choir of the communal. Our wilderness time does not shrink our boundaries but expands them, taking us to new depths and breadths and heights. We envision a new world, and—created in God's image and empowered through God's love—we have a part in shaping that world.

We use many images to talk about God's love for us. One image comes from Native American spirituality—that of Grandfather. A grandparent delights in a grandchild, offering a relationship of unconditional love, whispering love in many ways and languages all around the world: "You are beloved." Another image is that of Parent. When grown children return home, a father or mother rushes forward to meet them and throws loving arms around them. We are God's grown children, and when we venture forth in the wilderness to return to God with all our heart, God comes to meet us. It is like moving toward a candle at midnight. The flame of God shines in the darkness. As we move toward that light, a wonderful thing happens: the light begins to move toward us! When we open ourselves to that holy glow, we each glimpse faith's transforming vision of the person God created us to be—loved and loving, healed and healing, reconciled and reconciling—the person we can still become.

This journey of the heart toward God is both personal and communal. Joel says to "call a solemn assembly; gather the people. Sanctify the congregation." To sanctify something is to make it holy, to consecrate it to God, and to remove it from the profane or secular. Ezekiel tells us how God sanctified the house of Israel:

> I will sprinkle clean water upon you, and you shall be clean from all your uncleannesses, and from all your idols I will cleanse you. A new heart I will give you, and a new spirit I will put within you; and I will remove from your body the heart of stone and give you a heart of flesh.
>
> —Ezekiel 36:25-26

How can Ezekiel's words become real to contemporary communities of faith? First of all, the congregation would be cleansed symbolically from its impurities and idols. I don't think that Ezekiel had in mind forming a cleansing committee or hiring a consultant or recording congregational sins on newsprint with red and blue markers. I am reminded of Zooey's conversation with Mrs. Glass in J. D. Salinger's *Franny and Zooey*:

> I don't want you to go away with the impression that there's any—you know—any inconveniences involved in the religious life. I mean a lot of people don't take it up just because they think it's going to involve a certain amount of nasty application and perseverance—you know what I mean. . . . As soon as we get out of the chapel here, I hope you'll accept from me a little volume I've always admired. . . . "God Is My Hobby."

The "Zooey syndrome" is not uncommon in congregations, and it results in getting the body without the heart. Perhaps an appropriate contemporary image of congregational cleansing is to wash away its "God-is-my-hobby" expectations and commitments, to soak its stains and smash its idols, to be shaken by new habits of spiritual discipline. Congregational cleansing might involve sticking that word *repentance* in between *confession* and *forgiveness*, applying the scriptures to our congregational life. Cleansing may require perseverance in following the teachings of Jesus in a "Zooey syndrome" world that shuns sacrifice and servanthood, a world that honors greed and power.

Our congregation also would receive a heart transplant. We recall that in the Hebrew Scriptures the heart represents the whole. The heart of our congregation is the center from which its emotions, understanding, and devotion stem. It is the source from which wisdom, discernment, and obedience flow. The congregation's heart—the center of its being and doing—would not be a heart of stone.

And finally, with that new heart would come a new spirit. When Ezekiel spoke of "a new spirit," I don't think he was talking about circling the sanctuary while holding hands and getting a tingly feeling with perhaps a tear or two. Nor was he speaking about a catharsis in the candlelight and an endorphin release—or even about a sudden rush of joy and basking in benevolence. These things may happen, but they are by-products not goals.

One way to translate this "new spirit" for a contemporary congregation is by adapting the work of Edwin Friedman in *Generation to Generation*. He applies family systems theory to congregational systems, for he has found that the dynamics in family relationships also hold for church relationships. He talks about "differentiation"—the capacity to define our own goals and values apart from surrounding pressures. He says differentiation "includes the capacity to maintain a (relatively) nonanxious presence in the midst of anxious systems"; it "means the capacity to be an 'I' while remaining connected."

I want to carry Friedman's concept a step further (admittedly, further than he would have intended but appropriate for the purpose of envisioning a sanctified contemporary congregation). This "new spirit" would enable our congregation as a body (the congregational "I") to differentiate itself from the world—to define its own goals and values apart from secular pressures. The congregation would also be a nonanxious presence in the midst of the secular anxiety around it. This presence would base its existence on a strengthening visionary trust in God rather than a Pollyanna blindness. The congregation would not withdraw from the secular world but remain connected with it. In other words, this new spirit would enable our congregation to differentiate itself *from* the world so that it is centered upon God with wholehearted devotion, while simultaneously remaining connected missionally *to* the world.

Nouwen in his book *Here and Now* speaks of "a human family infinitely bound by God who created us to share, all of us, in the divine light." In our congregational pilgrimage to return to God with all our heart, the flash of divine light sparks our own small candles. We carry them into the world, aflame together as a congregation, bringing the light of God's healing and reconciling love into the secular midnight.

FORGIVENESS AND TRANSGRESSION

Scripture: Psalm 51:1-12

Like Ezekiel, the psalmist lifts up the heart and the spirit, but the focus is personal rather than corporate: "Create in me a clean heart, O God, and put a new and right spirit within me" (Psalm 51:10). Lent is a season for self-examination; it is not a time to waste energy sloshing around in guilt. The psalmist's prayer moves us beyond simply admitting our transgressions and asking for forgiveness.

The desert mothers and fathers of the third through sixth centuries help us take a deeper look at what it means to have a clean heart and a new spirit. According to Roberta Bondi in *To Love as God Loves*, they did not dwell on sins but on the *passions*, a word that had a very different meaning for them than it does for us today. The chief characteristics of a passion were the "perversion of vision and the destruction of love." Evagrius Ponticus distinguished himself as a theologian at the Second Ecumenical Council in 381. He analyzed the human soul and was the first to catalogue the eight passions: gluttony, avarice (greed), depression (sadness), lust, anger, acedia (restless boredom, sloth), vainglory (dependency upon praise or recognition), and pride. The desert mothers and fathers saw these

I. WIN - 8

passions as attitudes and feelings that needed healing. From this perspective, our sins are symptoms of our poor habits of the heart.

Abba Poeman, a desert father whose name means "the Shepherd," says that the passions work in four stages: "first, in the heart; secondly, in the face; thirdly, in words; and fourthly, . . . in deeds."[3] He says that we should "purify" the heart. For me, a passion is like an infection in our heart; if an infection is not healed or at least isolated, it spreads. First it spreads to our countenance. Time draws lines on the face that are a map of the heart. We've all seen kind faces and hard faces. What is hidden in our heart is open to the public. If the passion reaches this second stage and affects our facial expression, Abba Poeman warns us to "take care" not to let it affect our speech. If our infection advances to stage three, we begin to expose others to our dis-ease through hurtful words. Abba Poeman says that if the passion reaches this third stage, we must "cut the conversation short" to avoid the fourth stage of rendering "evil for evil." At this final stage of the infection, our behavior is destructive and harmful to others.

My experience as a counselor has taught me that we do not have to wait until our heart heals to form new habits; in fact, new habits can help us heal our heart. We can move backward, from behavior to source—from deed to heart. Once we are aware of the symptom and have a desire to work toward healing, discipline and practice can help bring change (like doing physical therapy exercises, driving golf balls, or practicing a piece of music brings improvement). If our passion—our infection of the heart—has advanced to the fourth stage, we can practice changing our behavior. For example, since *Mardi Gras* is over and Lent invites me to unmask, I will confess that vainglory is an affliction for me. I can practice moving off center stage, standing aside when it's time for recognition and not competing with others for praise. In time, with disciplined practice, we can back the passion out of our actions.

We can practice changing our language also, including changing the language of our thoughts. (I can hush that inner voice that whispers, *Did I do OK?*) Eventually, again with enough disciplined practice, we can back the passion out of our words. Lent is a season

✗ That's ME.

to unmask before God and self; and as trust builds, to unmask before others.

Our hearts cannot receive healing while we drain our energy to preserve a mask that we pretend hides our passion. When we bring new habits of behavior and language to our table talks with God and lay aside our self-deluding masks, we open ourselves to God's transformation of our hearts.

As we wander through the wilderness, struggling with transgression and forgiveness, with our "passions" and the healing of the heart, we plead along with the psalmist: "Do not cast me away from your presence, and do not take your holy spirit from me."

FREEDOM AND TRANSCENDENCE

Scripture: 2 Corinthians 5:20–6:2

To return to God with all our heart is not a pilgrimage that requires a rigid jaw, gritted teeth, and all our willpower. Instead it is a journey fueled by the transcending power of God's love. It was Love that looked upon the cross and birthed resurrection. That same Love frees us from poor habits of the heart and takes us from death to new life. Paul says, "See, now is the acceptable time; see, now is the day of salvation!"

Recently I participated in a retreat led by Roberta Bondi. One of the significant things she said was that, according to the desert fathers and mothers, God's love for us as persons is a "for-who-you-are" kind of love, not an "in-spite-of" kind of love.

Immediately my mind went back in time to the night I experienced this kind of love. For years (even in high school), each night before I went to sleep I reflected on all the things I'd done wrong that day. But one night (by then I was a mother with four children!), almost like a revelation, it occurred to me to stop that recounting and instead to pray—to thank God for the things I'd done right that day. I cannot explain what happened. Perhaps God was bored with my long and everlasting lists of wrongs—I was certainly tired of them. Perhaps it was all those sermons I'd heard my husband preach on grace. What I do know is that I felt God's "for-who-you-are" love, and I experienced a wonderful, joyful transformation that turned my life right side up.

If we perceive God's love as an "in-spite-of" kind of love, we have a sense of God's shining a glaring spotlight on our shortcomings; we slink into the shadows. But if we perceive God's love as a "for-who-you-are" kind of love, we have a sense of God's sharing a candle in the darkness. Our souls sing out to the Lord in the beautiful words of the Spanish hymn "Tú Has Venido a la Orilla," *sonriendo has dicho mi nombre* ("while smiling [you] have spoken my name").

Let's look at this for-who-you-are concept of love in terms of marriage. Suppose my spouse says to me, "I love you *because* of all you do for me." That leaves me feeling that I have to earn his love. Or suppose my spouse says, "I love you *despite* your shortcomings." That leaves me feeling judged not loved; it is condescending, not caring. But suppose my spouse says, "I love you *for who you are*." Now, *there's* a love I want to return!

Let's carry the marriage metaphor another step. The church is the bride of Christ. God's holy love for the church is not a *because* love and, therefore, dependent upon what a congregation does for God or for God's people in the name of Jesus Christ. It is not a *despite* love, evoking congregational guilt for its many shortcomings. God gives a *for-who-you-are* love to the congregation. This love is a freeing love—a powerful, transcending love that lifts us toward who we can become as persons created by God.

Let's take this one more step. Lent provides us a special opportunity to reflect on what kind of love we have for God. Perhaps we offer God a *because* kind of love: We love God *because* we might be rewarded for it or *because* we might be punished if we don't love God. Perhaps we offer God a *despite* kind of love: With a heavy sigh we muster up love for God *despite* the things we blame God for—our life situation, a natural disaster, or the loss of a loved one. But perhaps with overflowing, grateful hearts as persons and congregations, we offer God a *for-who-You-are* kind of love, worshiping and praising the incomprehensible yet personal, immanent yet transcendent, all-powerful yet all-loving Creator and Grandparent whom we humbly call God.

When I sat at the table in the presence of my family on *Mardi Gras* night, I knew I was loved with a *for-who-you-are* kind of love, and I joyfully returned that love to them. When we come to the table to be present with God, personally and communally, we can be confident that God loves us with this same kind of love. That is amazing! That is a miracle! *That* is a love we want to return!

[handwritten margin notes: Practicing Piety / Fasting]

FACADE AND TREASURE

Scripture: Matthew 6:1-6, 16-21

Jesus said, "For where your treasure is, there your heart will be also." The Lenten journey in the wilderness offers an opportunity to reflect on our treasure, for wherever it is, our heart (the center of our being and doing) is there also. *[handwritten: — what is my Treasure?]*

A family Easter tradition when our children were small was to color Easter eggs on Saturday and then hide them in the backyard Easter Sunday afternoon. As the children found the eggs, they put them in their Easter baskets. Each child took a turn hiding the brightly colored eggs for the others to find. One Easter, an egg was hidden so well it wasn't found. It wasn't even missed. It remained hidden, forgotten—until it rotted and the smell from the dryer vent got our attention!

As adults we continue the hunt. We accumulate trinkets for our baskets and hide them away without remembering that the joy in hiding something is seeing another's joy in finding it. We may hide a trinket so well that we forget about it, or our baskets may be so full we don't even miss it. The trinket collects dust in the darkness, unappreciated by us and unavailable to anyone else. There's nothing necessarily wrong with accumulating trinkets, but we can be so absorbed by them that they become the center of our being and doing, our treasure, where our heart is. Trinkets decorate the self; they do not deepen the spirit. When we feel empty, we seek more trinkets—but the spiritual void remains.

Some of us treasure our "personage." The Swiss psychiatrist Paul Tournier said that we are both "person" and "personage." When I think of "person," I think of authenticity and essence. "Personage," on the other hand, calls to mind appearance, image, facade. To some degree, our personage is our packaging. This struggle between person and personage is not new. Blaise Pascal, a seventeenth-century French religious philosopher and scientist, wrote, "We strive continually to adorn and preserve our imaginary self, neglecting the true one."

Public piety may be part of our packaging. We flaunt it before others, quoting scripture with impure motives, broadcasting our fasting, tooting our trumpet when we donate our trinkets. This public piety is merely one of the many dramatic roles played by our personage. Jesus warns us against this false piety. There is nothing wrong with a personage, but we can become so focused on the packaging, on the wrappings that cover our person (the original creation of the Creator), that our personage becomes the center of our being and doing, our treasure, where our heart is. When we feel empty, we add another layer of wrapping paper—but the spiritual void remains.

Some of us treasure our home. We enjoy making it pretty and sharing it with others who will appreciate it. Our home is a place that reduces the size of our world to a small enough space that we can feel important and be the one around whom it revolves. There's nothing wrong with enjoying our home, but we can be so concerned with it that it becomes the center of our being and doing, our treasure, where our heart is. When we feel empty, we buy a new chair or redecorate—but the spiritual void remains.

Some of us treasure our work. It is the first thing we think of when we open our eyes and our last thought before we go to sleep. There is nothing wrong with hard work, but we can be so consumed by it that it becomes the center of our being and doing, our treasure, where our heart is. When we feel empty, we work even harder—but the spiritual void remains.

Some of us treasure family. For all of us, family is special. Our loved ones enrich our lives and give us precious memories. But no matter how much we love them and throw ourselves into their well-being (or expect them to throw themselves into our well-being), we cannot do for them—nor they for us—what only God can do. Certainly there's nothing wrong with loving our families, but we can become so obsessed with family that it becomes the center of our being and doing, our treasure, where our heart is. When we feel empty, we throw ourselves even more intensely into family (or expect the same of them)—but the spiritual void remains.

When we return to God with all our heart, God fills our spiritual void and our perspective changes. We serve our families by bestowing God's *for-who-you-are* kind of love upon them and showing them how that love extends to all God's people. Our work becomes a channel of ministry, a vocation in which we reflect God's healing and reconciling love in our workplace. We welcome God to the table in our home. In those table talks we learn that through God's love we can be at home anywhere in God's world, and we feel no need for things to revolve around us. We risk transparent packaging and reach into the core of our being to become the person God created. We see trinkets as a means of giving rather than an end purpose for living. Our treasure is God.

Jesus' words fit congregations as well as individuals. A congregation's heart—the center of its being and doing—is where its treasure is. Some congregations treasure their image (high church, low church; contemporary church, good old-fashioned church). Some treasure their building (let's not share it with anyone who might get it dirty). Some congregations treasure their work beyond the walls—missional or evangelistic (and perhaps feel a bit smug about it). Some treasure the church family (let's not grow because it's a close family, and everyone thinks alike). Some treasure their pastor. There is nothing wrong with caring about our congregational image, or building and grounds, or missional and evangelistic work, or church family, or pastor. The problem arises when any of these dimensions becomes the center of a congregation's being and doing. At that point, it offers a fraudulent faith rather than a holistic one in which the congregation centers its heart on God.

When God is our treasure, personal and communal Easter egg hunts change. We share the contents of our baskets rather than hiding, hoarding, or forgetting about them till they rot. When our heart is with God, our vision as individuals and as congregations is filtered through a new lens. We envision a future healed and reconciled by God's love. That love empowers us to be among the healers and reconcilers who help transform our small space into God's holy community.

AT THIS CHAPTER'S OPENING, I left my family wandering in the wilderness, worried about being lost and longing for a compass. With gray moods matching the dimming gray light of dusk, we finally saw a place to set up camp that second night—small, but the only space we'd found that was not too steep and where the trees weren't too close together. We worked together, dreading the isolation that pressed in upon us—wondering silently where we were, yearning for the certainty we had left behind.

Our son Dirk chose the place to build the fire. Somberly he brushed aside spruce needles and encircled the space with stones. Then he made a small hollow in the rocky soil.

And in that moment I heard his voice reverberate through the wilderness, "A *compass!*"

Impossible!

"I found a *compass!*" Dirk lifted his hand, and in it he held an old, encased, army-green *working* compass!

WE ARE THE *LAOS*, the people of God. As persons and as communities of faith, we wander through the wilderness, trying to return to God with all our heart, yet feeling lost and longing for a compass. But when we pause in our pilgrimage and somberly brush aside our personal and cultural trappings, encircle our life space with gratitude, and peer into that small hollow at the core of our being, we rediscover old truths:

✧   Eternally, God's love penetrates our facades and abounds for us just as we are.

✧   Eternally, Jesus Christ is our Savior and Teacher even in a world that seeks false treasure.

✧ Eternally, the Holy Spirit abides with us, a dancing flame in the midnight darkness.

And in that moment our voices reverberate through the wilderness: "The *compass*! We have found the *compass*!"

Thoughts and Reflections

✧

- ✧ Name some times when you have felt in need of a spiritual compass. To whom or to what did you go? What comforted you? What gave you direction? *I was too ashamed & lost to ask direction.*
- ✧ What new learnings have you gained about the traditions of Lent? *Just by reviewing gibes me new energy*
- ✧ Joel 2:12 speaks of the journey of the heart to God as both an individual and a corporate act. Looking at your personal Lenten journey, how do you feel your heart being drawn to God? How do you expect transformation in your life? *Here I am, Take me*
- ✧ Consider church transformation and think of your church. What if your church were to receive a new heart? What might happen as a result of that congregational transformation of heart?
- ✧ Our understanding of love affects the ways we respond to love. How does a for-who-you-are understanding of love differ from an in-spite-of understanding of love? How can that different understanding help you in the times when you need a spiritual compass?
- ✧ The section on transgression describes eight passions as attitudes or feelings that need healing. Think about the position of these attitudes in your own life. How does your awareness of the presence of God heal these attitudes?
- ✧ Think about the distinction between essence and appearance in the section on treasure. What do you treasure? What does your congregation treasure? What does your church (denomination) treasure? What are the differences between the essence and the appearance of these treasures? How can your treasures help you serve in ministry?

2

Wanderers Called by Christ

$\diamond$

1n *Wouldn't Take Nothing for My Journey Now*, Maya Angelou tells the story of Annie Johnson, who reviewed her life journey and made a change: "I looked up the road I was going and back the way I come, and since I wasn't satisfied, I decided to step off the road and cut me a new path." During the Lenten season of self-evaluation and spiritual renewal, we look at the highway up ahead and glance back in the rearview mirror. Not satisfied with our journey, we too step off the road. We venture into the wilderness to break a new trail, Lenten wanderers called by Christ.

As we wander in the wilderness, one of the things that becomes clear to us is the superficiality of our relationships with God and with people. "Superficiality is the curse of our age," says Richard J. Foster in *Celebration of Discipline*, and the spiritual disciplines "call us to move beyond surface living into the depths." Our spiritual journey is three-dimensional—a venture inward, a venture outward, and a corporate venture through our community of faith. These spiritual adventures draw us into a deeper relationship with God, whose divine love can transform us, healing our poor habits of the heart.

SOLITUDE

Scripture: Luke 4:1-2, 5-9

Our venture inward begins with solitude. Luke tells us that when Jesus entered the wilderness, the tempter showed him all the kingdoms of the world in a vision and offered him their glory and also authority over them: "If you, then, will worship me, it will all be yours." Jesus answered him, "It is written, 'Worship the Lord your God, and serve only him.'"

A daily time of solitude strengthens us against the temptations of greed and power and reminds us that it is God we worship and serve. In *The Way of the Heart* Henri J. M. Nouwen says, "Without solitude we remain victims of our society and continue to be entangled in the illusions of the false self." This time of solitude gives us an opportunity to read the scriptures, reflect, meditate, pray, and listen. The Light seeks us, but our desire for darkness encourages us to hang back in the shadows. We resist being present to Presence.

We feel too busy, too fragmented, too weary to add anything else to our day, and yet that very fragmentation and weariness attest to our soul's crying out for solitude. In his *Long Rules* Saint Basil the Great, a fourth-century Cappadocian who received his earliest spiritual training from his saintly grandmother Macrina, said that "a secluded and remote habitation" contributes "to the removal of distractions from the soul." *Makes sense.*

Many of us do not have daily access to secluded and remote space. We live with overcrowding, overstimulation, and far too many choices. Sensory stimuli invade the walls of our homes—the sounds of traffic, jets overhead, heating and cooling systems, the TV, the visual noise of undone taxes and unpaid bills, the cooking smells that drift in from the neighbors. We learn to tune them out.

The spiritual discipline of solitude begins with deciding on a time and choosing a place—perhaps a small corner of a room. As we center on God in that space, we expand our senses rather than shutting them down. We come to the table to be present to God, opening our deaf ears and closed eyes, longing for wholeness and refreshment. In *The Breath of God* Nancy Roth speaks of creating a "holy spaciousness," time spent with God that is "not merely a part of the day but . . . the *center* of the day." The discipline of solitude does not produce instant spiritual depth; yet in the practice of solitude we gradually become aware of a shifting within us.

For me, it seems that if I provide the quantity of time, the quality will be provided. When I am home, I sit in a corner of my study by the east window before the sun rises. I curl my feet up on the sofa, sometimes with a cup of tea in hand. If it's cold, I cozy a quilt around me. I read a scripture passage and a bit from another book, followed by a time of prayer and silence.

My part is merely to show up at the table, unmasked before God and myself. During this table talk, the first colors of dawn peek through the pine trees and gradually streak the canvas as the Creator paints a new day. Yet somehow, this Creator who is active in the world is also present with me. In *The Other Side of Silence* Morton Kelsey writes, "Our part is mostly to accept the hand already stretched out to us." With both difficulty and joy, I allow myself to believe that the all-powerful, omniscient, holy God is that all-loving, personal, holy One whose hand is stretched out to me.

When I am away from home, excuses abound to cheat myself of this time of solitude. The Creator, of course, still paints the sky as the sun comes up—a constant no matter where I am. And I can still read a scripture passage and pray. But in a strange place I find it hard to show up at the table centered and undistracted.

For example, I had entered into this writing project, opening myself as a conduit for God's love. But while working on this portion, something happened. My clay feet stumbled. For two weeks and a day I struggled to write about solitude while feeling distant, fragmented, and uncentered. Anxiety about meeting the deadline piled up like trash, closing the conduit. I awoke one night—in the midnight darkness we all know—with words ticking in my mind like a clock spinning toward the deadline:

> *The time is passing. The page is blank.*
> *The time is passing. The page is blank.*
> *The table is empty.*

I tried to still the words and return to the Source. Suddenly I realized that during these fifteen days I'd worked on "Solitude" in the car, on a plane, and in a bus. I had slept in ten different places and eaten at thirty-some different tables. I recalled the advice of Richard Foster in *Celebration of Discipline*, "It is best to have one designated place rather than hunting for a different spot each day" and the words of Henri Nouwen in *Here and Now*: "Traveling is seldom good for the spiritual life." In that moment of grace, the Comforter came like a warm quilt and wrapped my disheveled soul in loving silence.

======= ✧ =======

FINDING A PLACE FOR SOLITUDE is difficult when we are away from home. However, Foster goes on to remind us that solitude is "not first a place but a state of mind and heart." We can be away from "home" even when we sit in our designated place—for we can come to the table uncentered in our faith, fragmented by demands, and distanced by worry about work or finances or a loved one. Just as these things steal moments from our time of solitude, so we can steal moments of solitude from other times of the day, entering into that centered space of healing and trust as necessity or opportunities arise.

When we set aside time and space for solitude, not only is our schedule changed, but our life is also rearranged. Solitude is like breathing in the Spirit, drawing fresh breath that we cannot hold forever but offer back to our small part of the hurting world. Thomas Merton wrote, "It is in deep solitude that I find the gentleness with which I can truly love [others]."[1] We come to the table, detaching ourselves from cultural confusion in order to attach ourselves to God more deeply and to other persons more freely.

SCRIPTURE

Scripture: Romans 10:8-13

Abba Moses was a released slave who turned to the desert late in life and became one of the great fathers of Scetis. He said, "Travellers who miss their way are still tiring themselves though they are walking no nearer to their destination."[2] Scriptures help us find our way in the wilderness. However, we are tempted to rush through scripture reading—going through the motions, allowing our minds to wander, thinking about the "to do" list for the day. We miss the way when we travel through the scriptures with our eyes and not our hearts.

Reading scripture is generally an individual, silent act for us today because we have access to our own Bibles. We seldom think about how our reading of scripture differs from the practice of the early church. Prior to Johannes Gutenberg's invention of printing with movable type in the mid-fifteenth century, books were copied by hand, and they were very scarce and expensive. During the first millennium and a half of Christianity, reading was essentially a corporate act of listening rather than a private act of looking. The word was not seen but proclaimed. The ears, not the eyes, were primary. Paul says, "The word is near you, on your lips and in your heart." With no family Bibles, Christians repeated the phrases and passages of scripture they heard in order to hold them in their hearts and have access to them in their minds.

Repetition remains one of the meaningful ways to read scripture today. In *Spiritual Traditions for the Contemporary Church*, Gabriel O'Donnell tells us about *lectio divina*—reading for holiness, reading in the quest for God. Rather than being a method of Bible study with the purpose of reading for comprehension or learning more about the Bible, *lectio divina* is a disciplined form of devotion.

To practice *lectio,* we find a private place and begin to repeat a text quietly and peacefully, to "mumble" it and "ponder it, rest in it." The point of this repetition is not so much for memorization as to allow the word of God to nourish us and to permeate our being. Once we store the text in memory, we may access it wherever we are. O'Donnell warns against random selections and suggests consecutive reading, picking up each day where we left off the previous day so that we experience continuity. How far along we get is less important than opening ourselves to the power of the text and lingering over a word or phrase that strikes us. We allow ourselves—through its repetition—to be drawn into it and to discover its meaning. The early monks and nuns approached *lectio* with devotion and expectation, believing that each text held a personal, immediate message from God. We, like they, come to the table to be with God, lingering over God's word, not letting our clay feet lead us into setting the agenda.

Whereas those who practice *lectio divina* recommend consecutive reading, Nouwen finds that reading the prescribed text for the day is a meaningful experience. He records in *Here and Now* that it has been "of immense spiritual value" to read a Gospel passage each morning: "to look at it and listen to it with my inner eyes and ears. I have discovered that when I do this over a long period of time, the life of Jesus becomes more and more alive in me and starts to guide me in my daily activities." This disciplined and holistically attentive reading also helps us find our way in the wilderness.

Another meaningful method of reading scripture is to look for levels of meaning. Early in the fifth century, John Cassian wrote that in addition to the literal meaning, scripture had three different spiritual levels: the tropological (which carries the moral meaning), the allegorical (which points to a deeper mystery), and the anagogical (which raises the mind to heaven).[3] This kind of reading encourages us to look behind the words and seek the multidimensional meanings of a passage—the moral, the mysterious, and the transcendent.

Ignatius of Loyola, a Spaniard born in 1491, provides us with another way to read the scriptures. Two of his exercises in *The Spiritual Exercises of Saint Ignatius* are reflective meditation and contemplation. In reflective meditation we place ourselves mentally in the presence of God through a scripture, asking: "*Who* is this speaking to me? *What* does this mean to me? *Where* does this apply to my life? *How* and *when* do I respond?"[4] We focus on how the specific scripture applies to our lives and trust that God will reveal this to us in the reflective process.

In the spiritual exercise of contemplation we prayerfully enter into the scriptural scene and participate in what is happening—seeing the images, smelling the odors and aromas, hearing the sounds. We open our senses and imagination and place ourselves in the situation. The "First Principle and Foundation" of Saint Ignatius expresses that "we are loved by God, gifted by God and called to use those gifts for God's greater glory." We strengthen this foundation when we engage ourselves in scripture.

We may read scripture in many ways. Our motivation, attitude, and purpose are more important than our methodology. The scriptures are not something to *get* through but to *grow* through. One of the joys we receive from our private reading is hearing in worship a scripture we really *know*. For example, in preparing to write this book, I studied the traditional scriptures for Ash Wednesday (from Joel, Psalms, Second Corinthians, and Matthew). When my pastor read them at the Ash Wednesday service, I felt a soul-deep joy of recognition and sharing, of wholeness and oneness with the community of faith. They were "my" scriptures. I had read them, pondered them, knew them. Once again my life was empowered in both a corporate and a personal way by the word, within my community of faith and beyond it. Through daily reading, scripture helps us find our way in the wilderness, while becoming an intrinsic part of our lives.

SILENCE

Scripture: Psalm 130

An ancient expression is appropriate for our journey through the wilderness: "To be on pilgrimage is to be silent."[5] The silence we seek is a silence of the heart. We bring this kind of silence to our relationships and to our time of solitude.

Abba Arsenius, a learned man who left Rome for Scetis and became renowned for his silence and austerity, confessed, "I have often repented of having spoken, but never of having remained silent."[6] Words are a form of control. While people are speaking, they don't have to listen to anyone else, and they can maintain control of the conversation by continuing their ramblings, ravings, or righteous opinions. If they pause, they risk losing their opportunity to dominate. We see this in debates on television. We see it in meetings and social gatherings. We see it in ourselves. But as Dietrich Bonhoeffer reminds us in *Life Together*, "Real silence, real stillness, really holding one's tongue comes only as the sober consequence of spiritual stillness."

During the retreat I mentioned earlier, Roberta Bondi suggested that our friends would find our continuous monologues boring, and the same is true in our table talks with God. When we come to the table, we have permission to relax, to be who we are, and to share our joy, gratitude, and pain—as we do with any dear friend. It is also good to sit in silence with God and listen. The psalmist put it this way: "I wait for the Lord, my soul waits, and in his word I hope."

In his book *The Other Side of Silence*, Morton Kelsey describes prayer as listening to God. Yet we find it difficult to get a quiet mind. Distractions abound. We have to find our way through a maze of peripheral clutter to settle into silence, like making our way through a junky attic. Kelsey relates the experience of silence to that of being in the theater as we wait for our eyes to adjust to the dim lights and for the play to begin. Our task is to come to the table with open minds and hearts, trusting God with the process.

This silence at the table before God is somewhat like those rare and precious moments of silent communion with friends. One evening during Lent I sat with my friends Ann and Eleanor. We had been to the hospital on this painful day, offering a hug where words were too weak, praying for the critically ill one and her family, praying for that strength that God gives in times of need. Then, this afternoon, she had died—our sister in the United Methodist clergy family. And now, the three of us sat together at Ann's table, drawing comfort from one another's presence, lingering over tea late into the night, feeling that silent hungering for community that comes in times of loss. There was little talk. Words were inadequate and superfluous. Our silence together was a shared silence of the heart.

So it is in our silence at the table with God. Those moments of shared silence of the heart with God are moments of deep communion. We enter into that calm center where we feel differentiated from the world and connected to our Creator, and in the silence we hear the word of hope. Nouwen writes in *Here and Now*, "Once we come to know that inner, holy place, a place more beautiful and precious than any place we can travel to, we want to be there and be spiritually fed." When we rise from the table, the power of Presence empowers us to be present to others, not only in our words and deeds but also in the beautiful and holy communion of silence.

STUDY

Scripture: Genesis 2:4-9, 15-17, 25–3:7

The Bible is over a thousand pages, and we barely reach page three before the desire for instant wisdom gets God's children in trouble:

> So when the woman saw that the tree was good for food, and that it was a delight to the eyes, and that the tree was to be desired to make one wise, she took of its fruit and ate; and she also gave some to her husband, who was with her, and he ate.
>
> —Genesis 3:6

Instant wisdom! Since the beginning we've wanted to be wise without effort, without time, without that *S*-word we learned to dislike as children—*study*. Unfortunately, not a bite of an apple—or a byte of an Apple—gives us wisdom. The journey toward wisdom begins with the spiritual discipline of study, which alters our patterns of thought and thereby helps change our habits of the heart.

Eve listened to the tempter, who filled her mind with garbage. Computer programming offers a metaphor: *Garbage in; garbage out.* So it is with our minds. The tempter comes to us in the garbage of market mentality with its honor misplaced, greedy face, and money race. The tempter comes in the garbage of media mania with its skewed news, spewed anger, and sensational half-truths. The seeds we plant in our minds intentionally—or by being unintentional—determine the crop we reap: *Stinkweeds in; stinkweeds out.* Nouwen in *Here and Now* poses the question, "Do we really want our mind to become the garbage can of the world?"

The spiritual discipline of study sets us free. The words *library* and *liberty* come from the same Latin root *liber*, which means "free" or "book." The study of a good book nurtures our minds and hearts. It gives us something worthwhile to think about in limbo moments during the day—while walking, waiting in line, sitting in a traffic jam. We can study at home or take a book with us in our purse, briefcase, or lunch bag. Some of us may study a book a week or a

book a month. Some of us may prefer to spend ten minutes a day in disciplined study. Even giving ourselves one day off a week, that daily ten minutes mounts up to an hour a week, which is the equivalent of taking one half-day a month for study or three weekend study retreats a year.

The spiritual classics, the sayings of the desert fathers and mothers, and contemporary Christian writers help us along our journey. Study time differs from devotional time, and we need not limit our readings to Christian writers or fear gleaning wisdom from other great religions. Three criteria may help us in our study selection: 1) Will it nurture my mind and heart? 2) Will it help me to look at the world as God sees it? 3) Will it help transform my life as I journey in faith through today's world?

We need not limit study to books. Evelyn Underhill and Richard J. Foster commend the study of nature. It was in reading *Celebration of Discipline* a few years ago that I began to study a pine tree outside my window. Foster says that "the first step in the study of nature is reverent observation." Taking him seriously, I reverently observed that tree for several consecutive days as the sun came up. In the beginning I saw a beautiful old tree, but by the third day my mind had transformed the tree into an image of prayer. I noticed how the trunk rises into the air and divides, like the palms of two hands pressed together in prayer. That image is now part of my memory wherever I am. In the desert or over the sea, my mind gives me the gift of that tree: *Pine tree in; prayer tree out.* "The object of contemplation matters little," says Underhill in *Practical Mysticism.* "From Alp to insect, anything will do, provided that your attitude be right: for all things in this world towards which you are stretching out are linked together, and one truly apprehended will be the gateway to the rest."

The Genesis story continues, "Then the eyes of both were opened, and they knew that they were naked; and they sewed fig leaves together and made loincloths for themselves." These two in the garden had information, but they lacked wisdom. How like them we are! We "surf the net," pushing computer keys and accessing the facts on the information highway. We can use facts for control, and they can build arrogance, but they don't equal wisdom.

Through disciplined study, we learn to assimilate and analyze, comprehend and contemplate. We reach for the gift of discernment. Bonhoeffer reminds us: "There is meaning in every journey that is unknown to the traveler."[7] Each day has a story to tell us—through reading, nature, art, experiences, and relationships. Yet often we are open to facts and blind and deaf to the meaning of the journey!

Paul was aware of the garbage in the world and our need for mental alternatives. He reminded us that "whatever is true, whatever is honorable, whatever is just, whatever is pure, whatever is pleasing, whatever is commendable, if there is any excellence and if there is anything worthy of praise, think about these things" (Philippians 4:8). The spiritual discipline of study helps us renew our minds and focus our thoughts on these things.

Sanctified Fasting

Scripture: Matthew 4:1-4

The Gospel of Matthew records these words, "Then Jesus was led up by the Spirit into the wilderness to be tempted by the devil. He fasted forty days and forty nights." The spiritual discipline of fasting expands our inner awareness. However, fasting may be the most misinterpreted aspect of Lent. It has nothing to do with giving up chocolate (though for some of us this is more sacrificial than it might appear). To fast does not mean cutting out a snack in our overfed culture—or skipping breakfast or going on a crash diet. Joel tells us to "sanctify a fast" (2:15). To sanctify a fast is to make it holy; we remove it from the realm of the secular and consecrate it to God.

The Hebrew Scriptures depict two kinds of fasting—public and private—and prayer accompanies both. Humbling or afflicting oneself was synonymous with fasting. Frequently persons wore sackcloth as a sign of penance and mourning. Private fasts were observed not only as penance but also when others were sick.

The Gospels teach us that attitude and motive are important. Jesus spoke of joy in fasting and reminded us not to fast for appearances. (See Matthew 6:16-18.) The early church observed fasting during periods of severe difficulty as well as prior to the consecration of teachers and elders.

Fasting is a sacred act. In *Celebration of Discipline*, Foster writes, "Fasting must forever center on God." Only through this centering does skipping meals become a holy fast. To fast for others' attention, affirmation, or admiration defeats the purpose, which is to draw closer to God. When sanctified, our small sacrifices for Lent plunge us to a deeper level of self-knowledge, compassion, devotion, and gratitude.

Fasting from food is traditional and fundamental. Other kinds of fasts also expand our inner awareness and seem especially appropriate during our wilderness wanderings. We can fast from judging others, from focusing on differences, from worrying and complaining. We can fast from suspicion and anger and hostility. We can fast from pessimism and bitterness. These fasts, when taken seriously as holy acts, can be significant steps in returning to God with all our heart.

Inherent in a fast is a feast. When we fast from food, we feast on prayer and God's bountiful love. When we fast from divisive patterns of relating with others, we feast on the amazing awareness that each face we see is the face of Christ. When we fast from building social, economic, and political walls, we feast on our universal oneness with the One.

SIMPLICITY

Scripture: Psalm 91:1-2, 9-16

In *Celebration of Discipline* Foster tells us, "Simplicity is freedom." The clutter in our lives can block our perception of the presence of the ever-living, ever-loving Creator. The discipline of simplicity helps us remove the clutter and envision all life as a gift from God. Simplicity is not about possessions—neither having possessions nor lacking them—but about being possessed.

Through the discipline of simplicity we realize that accumulation possesses us—accumulation of things, honors, compliments. Indeed, our culture is possessed by possessions. Accumulation enslaves us whether our focus is on getting everything we want or on resenting those who do. When accumulation possesses us, our joy comes from hoarding rather than sharing. We pile our accumulated stuff in storage closets, storage rooms, storage sheds—and rent storage units for the overflow. We even forget what we have boxed up until the next time we move.

The more things we accumulate, the more anxiety we feel about protecting them. Possessed by possessions, we carry keys and remember codes; we buy insurance to pay for trouble before it comes; we have safes and security systems. How we clutter and complicate our lives!

Backpacking is a lesson in simplicity. We need a tent and a bedroll, a change of clothes, a bar of soap and a toothbrush, water and simple food, a pan for cooking and a pot for boiling, a pocketknife, and eating utensils. (And a compass!) That's all. When we backpack, we don't take more than we need. We share all that we have with one another. We enjoy things along the way without having to take them home with us. Carrying our possessions on our backs clears our vision as to how very little we actually *need*. Innate in simplicity is a quiet refusal to frame our lives in the gold gilt of greed.

Through the discipline of simplicity, we also become aware of our addiction to busyness. We invest huge chunks of irreplaceable time to earn enough money to buy all that stuff to put in all that storage space. Nifty little calendars and organizers steal our life day by day as surely as a judge's sentence. We forget that schedules belong to us; we don't belong to them.

We thank people for "taking time" from their "busy schedule." We zip through life like we zip through a revolving door, going faster and faster around in circles. We run on digital time—not analog time. No friendly round face of the clock for us, with those hands that settle for "approximately." Our cluttered lives demand wrist alarms with faceless time, precise time, digital time. *Now! Now! Now!*

Possessed by schedules, we content ourselves with a frantic frenzy that reflects our inner fragmentation. A schedule that comes from the clarity of a heart centered on God may look as busy as before, but the schedule comes from prayerful consideration. We reflect a calm inner wholeness, and in that wholeness we *give* time to others rather than *take* time for them.

The image that helps me get in touch with the discipline of simplicity is a white-out. I experienced a white-out one night while driving from Denver to Colorado Springs. The interstate closed after I was already on it, and the world turned white. I crept along on a coat of ice covered with snow. Huge flakes, unleashed and wild, blew into my windshield. They swirled, blinded, mesmerized. All of creation merged together in whiteness. I could not distinguish one thing from another—not the road, not the median or the shoulders, not the exits or entry lanes. For over two hours that night I slowly inched along through limbo, the world around me freed from clutter. It was not only the dangerous drive that scared me but also the formlessness—as though my cluttered life itself was suddenly blank, in limbo, waiting to be reformed.

The discipline of simplicity teaches us how to come to the table in a white-out before God—dis-possessed, free from clutter. In this white-out we get a fresh start. We choose to put back into our lives only the essentials and to add things previously ignored that faith now calls forth. In our white-out before God we feel trust, not anxiety; we "live in the shelter of the Most High" and "abide in the shadow of the Almighty" and "say to the Lord, 'My refuge and my fortress; my God, in whom I trust.'" In our white-out before God we re-form our lives in an attitude of gratitude. We sit at the table with a deep thankfulness that wells up inside us and overflows.

Simplicity is not about living *without*; it is about living *with*. Living with God's good earth, with God's creatures, with all God's people. It is about living with gratitude for God's amazing gift of life. The discipline of simplicity clears our vision, and we can stand with David in James Michener's *The Fires of Spring*, who had "seen and listened and touched and smelled and tasted with love, and the treasure trove was with him forever."

SERVICE

Scripture: Deuteronomy 26:1-11

In *Celebration of Discipline* Foster concludes the chapter on service by suggesting the following: "Begin the day by praying: 'Lord Jesus, I would so appreciate it if You would bring me someone today whom I can serve.'" This simple prayer gets at the heart of the discipline of service. However, it is a dangerous prayer when prayed genuinely. Those words—*I would so appreciate it if You would bring me someone today whom I can serve*—change the direction of our clay feet.

I would so appreciate it. Our growth in the discipline of service turns appreciation upside down. Appreciation is expressed by the server rather than expected of the served. We don't reach down patronizingly from our perch on the ladder "to help this poor little person"; as children of God we all stand on the same rung. We don't put the other in our debt, instilling a sense of obligation or ringing up points for collection; our service is a gift. We don't serve with a stifled sigh of duty, followed later by complaints to a friend (or bragging subtly about our goodness); service itself is a source of joy. We are simply and silently grateful for the opportunity to serve.

If You would bring. Through the discipline of service we learn to view the person we serve as one brought to us by the Lord. Our service, therefore, is a way of responding in love to God's manifest love for us. "So now I bring the first of the fruit of the ground that you, O Lord, have given me." We do not hurriedly share a piece of leftover pie; we bake a fresh one with the "first fruit"—and give the whole thing without holding back. We do not serve for reward, for applause or admiration or with the secret hope of financial gain; our service leads to a sense of abundant life within us.

Me. My presence? But I have books to write (or a ladder to climb or a ten-year plan to achieve). How about just contributing money? Or talking about it at the next meeting of the church missions committee? Or sending the pastor? After all, that's the person who's paid to serve. In *Life Together* Bonhoeffer speaks of "simple assistance in trifling, external matters" and suggests, "One who worries about the loss of time that such petty, outward acts of helpfulness entail is usually taking the importance of his [or her] own career too solemnly." Service is more than donating, discussing, or delegating—it is *doing!*

Someone. Through the discipline of service we grow toward recognizing the face of Christ in each person we serve; therefore, we do not pass judgment on who deserves our gift and who does not.

Catherine de Hueck Doherty, the author of *Poustinia*, says that "every human face is also the icon of Christ." It is "only in identifying with Christ . . . that I can love and identify with others." We see each "someone"—near or far, renowned or unknown, liked or disliked—as a loved sister or brother.

Today. Pray for the opportunity to serve someone *today*? But we are trying to unclutter our lives. How about "someday" instead? Someday when we have more time or when our own problems aren't so big or when we are in the mood or when we aren't so weary. We might get burnout from all this daily service.

Nancy Roth, speaking of the Orthodox tradition of "*synergeia*—synergy, or cooperation with God" reminds us that if "we cooperate with God through using the energy and insight we have received in prayer, our prayer becomes action, and that action, in turn, becomes a form of prayer."[8] Isaiah put it another way:

> Those who wait for the Lord
> > shall renew their strength,
> > they shall mount up with wings like eagles,
> > they shall run and not be weary,
> > > they shall walk and not faint.
> > > > —Isaiah 40:31

Whom I can serve. We are not unlike Felicia in John Updike's *The Witches of Eastwick*, who had "a considerable love for the underprivileged in the abstract but when actual cases got close to her she tended to hold her nose." We would like to serve God in the abstract. We would like to fantasize some grand, noble gesture; a heroic and dramatic act significant enough for others to take notice and marvel. However followers of the Christ of the cross are not called to wait for the big event but to serve concretely in the small daily ways that go unnoticed. As we grow in the discipline of service, we become more faithful to that call.

The word of God is a word of love, and that Word comes to us in different disguises. Our prayer of the heart to be sent someone we can serve teaches us to listen for that Word in everyone we encounter and to look for that Word in each disguise. Mahatma Gandhi said, "The task of the true servant of society . . . is to prepare in interior silence and consecrated action a place for the future to be born."[9] Through the discipline of service we do our little bit to bring the holy community of God to our small space on the planet.

THE *POUSTINIA* IS A HELPFUL IMAGE for us as we wander through the wilderness with halos and clay feet. *Poustinia* is a Russian word meaning "desert, a lonely and silent place." It also means a place where people go to seek God in solitude. A *poustinik* was a religious pilgrim, a person called by God to go into the desert to live in prayer, silence, and simplicity—but always keeping one side of the *poustinia* open to the world in order to see the needs and to get there quickly to serve. So it is with us. Our small corner of the room we use for solitude is our *poustinia*, which we enter to grow in spiritual depth, always keeping a view open to the needs of the world so we can serve daily. Doherty says, "The *poustinia* is within, and one is forever immersed in the silence of God, forever listening to the word of God, forever repeating it to others in word and deed." Our *poustinia* ultimately becomes a place of the heart from which we focus on the sacred while serving in the world. The personal and corporate spiritual disciplines lead us—like Annie Johnson some years back—as we dare to cut a new path for our lives.

THOUGHTS AND REFLECTIONS

✧ This chapter describes seven aspects of spiritual life. How does thinking about these seven disciplines as holy habits change your understanding of Lent? Which discipline is most difficult for you? Which one would you like to practice more deeply? *Study*

✧ Do you set apart a special time and place for solitude? In what ways can you un-busy and un-clutter your life to allow more solitude in God's presence? *Give up T, V,*

✧ Have you ever experienced a powerful silent communion with God or with a friend or with nature? Offer thanks for that experience. If you are part of a group studying this book, you may wish to describe this experience to the group.

✧ What kind of study rhythm works best with your schedule? How comfortable do you feel with yourself as you contemplate? What must you overcome to be more comfortable in silent reflection before God? *I do - in my own reminising*

✧ Fasting often becomes a Lenten joke instead of a sacred act. What kind of fasting would help you? During the fast, in what specific ways can you better feast on prayer and God's love? Try to describe a fast, and a feast on prayer, that your church might adopt.

✧ Think about an ordinary week in your life, then finish this sentence: "If I could simplify my life, I would . . . " What clutters your life? What obstacles prevent you from simplifying your life? *thoughts of the past.*

✧ Do you feel joy when you serve others? How do others witness your joy? *Yes -*

3

Wanderers with Halos and Clay Feet

Others

Incorporate

Interesting phrase.

W e are wanderers in the wilderness with halos and clay feet. Jesus said, "Where two or three are gathered in my name, there am I in the midst of them" (Matthew 18:20, RSV).

Just as our personal venture keeps us from being strangers to the spiritual disciplines, our corporate venture keeps us from being lone rangers armed with the Bible and misfiring verses for our own vested interests. In *Life Together* Dietrich Bonhoeffer reminds us of the importance of both the personal and the corporate. "One who wants fellowship without solitude plunges into the void of words and feelings, and one who seeks solitude without fellowship perishes in the abyss of vanity, self-infatuation, and despair."

Which am I?   #2

CALLED TO COMMUNITY

Scripture: Psalm 27

The psalmist says: "One thing I asked of the Lord, that will I seek after: to live in the house of the Lord all the days of my life, . . . and to inquire in his temple." We are wanderers called to a community of faith.

~ 49 ~

In *Christianity Rediscovered* Vincent Donovan tells the story of teaching the Christian message to Ndangoya and his Masai community in East Africa. After a year of inquiring and learning they decided they wanted to become Christians. As the priest began to judge who qualified for baptism and who did not, Ndangoya interrupted him, saying,

> Padri, why are you trying to break us up and separate us? . . . Yes, there have been lazy ones in this community. But they have been helped by those with much energy. There are stupid ones in the community, but they have been helped by those who are intelligent. Yes, there are ones with little faith in this village, but they have been helped by those with much faith. Would you turn out and drive off the lazy ones and the ones with little faith and the stupid ones? . . . We have reached the step in our lives where we can say, "We believe."

We are believers. Our faith is a we-believe faith—a communal faith. As individual Christians we differ in our willingness, our devotion, our abilities. But in the community of faith, we can learn from one another, help one another, call forth the best in one another. Our corporate strength compensates for our individual weaknesses. *Together* we are the body of Christ.

CALLED TO CONFESSION

Scripture: Ephesians 2:4-10

We are wanderers with halos and clay feet, and we are called to confession. Especially during the Lenten season, we are to examine our personal and corporate conscience, honestly confess, and sorrowfully repent.

On the second Sunday in Lent, my husband and I visited a small congregation of mixed races, ages, and lifestyles in New Orleans. I could feel the sense of community as the people gathered. When it was time in the service for the "Young People's Message," an eighth-grade boy came forward comfortably, the only youth present. The pastor talked a bit about confession and then asked him, "What do young people your age need to confess?"

"Hating others," the boy began. "Saying bad things about people and cheating on tests."

Those things, I thought, *haven't changed.*

Then he added, "And it's a shame but sometimes sexual activity." He paused. "And sometimes, it's a shame, murder."

Kids killing kids—things have changed!

Later during congregational concerns, one member said he'd been laid off from his job and would have to move. Another lifted up concern for a friend dying of AIDS. A teacher expressed concern for a child at school whose parents had lost their income because a mass shooting in their café had driven business away. A man reverently said the name of the beloved neighborhood priest who'd been murdered that week. An "Amen" echoed softly through the sanctuary, and a prayer was offered for the priest's congregation Saints Peter and Paul Catholic Church.

We confess that we have much to learn from the Masai about community. The spiritual infrastructure of our society is in shambles. In *Dakota: A Spiritual Geography* Kathleen Norris says that she suspects that when modern Americans ask "What is sacred?" they are really asking "What community do I belong to?" She suggests that we are seeking "anything with strong communal values and traditions. But all too often we're trying to do it on our own, as individuals."

A sense of community has broken down throughout our country, and in that process the township, the neighborhood, and the family have crumbled. Parker J. Palmer, author of *The Company of Strangers*, notes that "a declining sense of self" accompanies the "declining sense of community in our society," which is "to be expected, since a sense of self comes from community." Through the community we offer one another and receive from one another both challenge and comfort.

The writer of Ephesians tells us that "God, who is rich in mercy, out of the great love with which he loved us even when we were dead through our trespasses, made us alive together with Christ—by grace you have been saved." As I sat in that New Orleans sanctuary, its windows wide open to the world on that beautiful spring morning, I felt the congregation's capacity for connectedness, their willingness to draw on one another's strengths and resources, and their readiness to hold one another accountable. The sirens down Rampart Street shrieked of sins—of those outside and those inside. And then the bells of the oldest cathedral in our country, Saint Louis Cathedral, tolled like grace, forgiving us. We are those who are alive *together* with Christ, believers finding hope and grace in our sacred community of faith.

CALLED TO CONVERSION

Scripture: 1 John 4:7-12

In *The Call to Conversion* Jim Wallis says, "Conversion means a radical reorientation in terms of personal needs and ideas of personal fulfillment. . . . Community is the environment which can enable that conversion, and community is the fruit of that conversion." Each of us can point to conversions that added new and undiscovered depth to our faith journey. To unmask ourselves and share these stories, without need for approval or fear of disapproval, can be a meaningful part of our Lenten wanderings together.

For me, three conversions stand out. The first occurred at home one night long ago when my husband Bill was in seminary in Massachusetts and was also serving an old New England congregation. He was at a meeting in the church across the street, and our baby was asleep upstairs. I was reading *Herein Is Love*.

I remember the moment exactly. I sat with my legs curled up in a green wingback chair in the high-ceilinged living room of the parsonage with its big drafty windows and wide-board floors, the gold *fleur-de-lis* wallpaper holding the hundred-year-old walls together, and the soothing aroma of a cup of jasmine tea on the oak table beside me. Though I was "alone," three of us formed my community that evening—Reuel Howe through his book and John the Elder through the scriptures: "Herein is love, not that we loved God, but that he loved us" (1 John 4:10, KJV).

Howe quoted the verse and followed it with these words: "Having given us His love, we have it for our response to Him, so that we love Him by loving one another. . . . Our responsibility is to love Him. We are to love God by loving one another, and in loving one another we introduce one another to God." As I read those words, suddenly like a blinding flash of light I knew, felt, experienced God's love for me. The Creator of the Universe, the Omniscient One, the All-Powerful and Almighty One, the Incomprehensible One of awesome mystery—that One loves *me*! I don't have to earn that love by being perfect. I can simply receive it. And gratefully return it. And joyfully share it with others. A silent *Hallelujah!* reverberated through my whole being. That night I passed through a door that turned my life toward deepened love.

My second major conversion occurred with 11,500 people at the Baton Rouge Centroplex beside the Mississippi River. We were United Methodists from all across Louisiana—a kaleidoscope of shifting color, from our clothes to the shades of our skin—one in the Spirit, gathered by the river to celebrate and worship God. On that glorious afternoon we renewed our baptismal vows. I can still feel that water on my forehead, the power of spiritual energy in that place, the vitality of our corporate renewal. The service closed by sending us into the world, led by a Native American lay pastor carrying a symbolic Houma cross, a New Orleans jazz band, a 500-member youth choir, and a 1,000-voice adult choir. As we joined together in "When the Saints Go Marching In," I knew, felt, experienced the empowerment of our faith *together*. I realized that if we open ourselves corporately to the power of the Spirit, we can indeed transform our own small space in God's world. That afternoon I passed through a door that turned my life toward deepened faith.

My third major conversion occurred in a gathering primarily of strangers on the other side of the planet during the final days of the U.S.S.R. I was in Ekaterinburg, the closed military industrial city called Sverdlovsk at that time. Having received the blessing of Archbishop Melkhisedek of the Russian Orthodox Church and also the permission of the city officials, we gathered as a worshiping community—a community whose governments had taught us to hate and fear one another. A community that included factory workers who'd made missiles to aim at the United States. A community with at least one member of the KGB. But we came together in the name of Christ. Excitement was contagious—the church had begun the year before, and tonight's service would close with baptism. The Russian Christians wanted all the beloved children baptized first for fear of the service's interruption or the rescission of permission to gather the next night. The Boys' Choir sang while over a hundred people crowded on the platform. Somehow little Giorgi broke loose from his parents and toddled toward my husband. Bill scooped him up and sat him on his knee. When the choir finished, little Giorgi was the first one baptized. As these wonderful people came forward courageously, I saw the light of holy joy in their eyes; and I knew, felt, experienced the Christ of reconciling, life-giving hope. That evening I passed through a door that turned my own life toward deepened hope.

Wallis says that through conversion, "Our perspective changes from 'what can the community do for me' to 'what can I do to best serve the community?'" These words sound old-fashioned in a culture where *me*-ism looks down its nose at *we*-ism. They are not intended to foster a style of service that pants to catch up due to a chronic disease of "yes"—that is not good stewardship of time and energy. Faithful service is a result of serious table talk in solitude and prayer so that our specific gifts match specific needs. As Christians, we are called to conversion—the passage that is not merely a change of opinion or even attitude but a change of direction.

CALLED TO COMPASSION

Scripture: Colossians 3:12-17

One misty evening when we lived in Oklahoma, I was waiting at home for Bill to finish at the church and pick me up for a Sunday school class party. I puttered about the kitchen, listening for the car. Suddenly I heard a crash at our corner. Afraid it was Bill, I shot out the door. Two unknown cars stood askew in the intersection. I called out through the mist, "Should I phone the police?"

"Yes," came the heavy answer.

"An ambulance?" The question sent a shiver through me.

"You'd better."

After the call I walked through the mist toward the cars. And then I saw her. A teenager was lying there on her back, thrown from the passenger door. Her head was on the curb. Her eyes were closed; her face serene, oblivious to the mist. I ran back into the house to get a blanket. The police arrived as I covered her. But the ambulance was very slow that night. Too slow. And the mist was falling.

She died on the way to the hospital without regaining consciousness. She was fifteen years old, and she and her uninjured friend, who was driving, were on their way to the Catholic church for youth group.

Some weeks later an insurance investigator came to talk to me. He introduced himself as Mr. Shanks and explained that he represented the car manufacturer and that the family was suing them for a faulty door. He sat in the den, his legal pad and pen in hand, asking me questions. After a while he said, "Well, what I can't figure out is why they would sue the company but not sue the driver."

I thought about that young driver, hysterical that night. How she would relive that evening, putting herself behind that wheel a thousand times again—but carefully stopping at that stop sign she'd missed, carefully watching for the speeder who'd come, carefully being sure her friend was buckled in. I looked at the investigator, sitting on the edge of his chair, a deep frown creasing his brow. "Maybe, Mr. Shanks, they feel compassion for her."

Shock unmasked his face. His jaw dropped. The hardness left his eyes. He leaned back in the chair, his whole countenance altered. He sat there in silence for a few moments and then spoke in a soft tone. "I—I'm sorry. In this line of work . . . I . . . I had forgotten about . . . compassion."

Sometimes we all forget about compassion. Paul says, "As God's chosen ones, holy and beloved, clothe yourselves with compassion." The word *compassion* derives from a Latin combination that means "to suffer with." To clothe ourselves with compassion is to suffer with others.

The menace to community today is that we stress what divides us rather than what brings us together. Instead of coming together as fellow travelers on the common human journey of birth, growth, giving birth, work, and death—filled with compassion for one another—we pass judgment on others as we walk by. As Henri Nouwen states in *The Way of the Heart*, "Compassion can never coexist with judgment because judgment creates the distance, the distinction, which prevents us from really being with the other." We create that distance as we alter our responses to others based on our subtle judgment (prejudice, prejudgment) of *more* or *less* (more capable or less capable, more responsible or less responsible, more powerful or less powerful). Some of us have little compassion for those we judge to be "less"; others of us have little compassion for those we judge to be "more." When we clothe ourselves with compassion, we close our eyes to differences and open our hearts to a sojourner's suffering. We *feel* the other's pain.

But feeling, by itself, is not enough. As Nouwen goes on to remind us, "Compassion is hard because it requires the inner disposition to go with others to the place where they are weak, vulnerable, lonely, and broken." Compassion is not merely a sympathy card. It offers an ear to hear the story, the time to walk together, and a touch of kindness along the way. Yet compassion is not a takeover by a do-gooder. It does not intrude on another's space, is never "in-your-face." It reaches out with respect and sensitivity.

The first part of the word *compassion* contains the word *compass*. Compassion gives us direction in the wilderness. Our faith journey is not a straight-line rocket launch into the heavens. Nor is it a AAA Triptik, marking the fastest route. If we clothe ourselves in compassion, we will experience a wandering journey with interruptions and digressions for other wanderers along the way. We will find that compassion *is* the route toward returning to God with all our hearts.

CALLED TO SANITY

Scripture: Ephesians 3:14-19

Abba Anthony said, "A time is coming when men will go mad, and when they see someone who is not mad, they will attack him saying, 'You are mad, you are not like us.'"[1] We live in a complex world where some people have gone mad, and many more are afraid not to be like them. We are called to sanity in the midst of this madness.

We see madness in our justice system. Lawsuits can be a source of fraud, with the greedy (a few unethical trios of "victim"-lawyer-doctor) conspiring together. In criminal justice, facts seem less relevant than legal loopholes, which skews the system toward the wealthy. Helen Prejean in *Dead Man Walking* cites comments about never finding the rich on death row because "the expert legal counsel they hire know how to 'play the system.'" Have we reduced the ancient symbol of blind justice to guilt and truth?

We see madness in our political system. Many lobbyists buy votes (a tax-deductible business expense). In a TV interview a retired lobbyist for a product that posed a health risk admitted that he had publicly attested to "facts" that he knew were lies. "But that wasn't illegal," he said. "I wasn't under oath." With no sign of remorse—not in his face, his eyes, or his tone—he added, "I was paid to lie. That was my job." For sale or trade: honor and integrity, ethical behavior, and moral character.

We see madness in our violence. In *EarthCurrents*, Howard A. Snyder paints a dismal portrait: "The United States has become Earth's most heavily armed and violent nation." In 1990, over 10,000 handgun murders occurred in our country, compared with 22 in Great Britain. We also now lead the world in the percentage of citizens behind bars, with the number of imprisoned women jumping in 1990 "about twice the rate for men." But the most dismal portrait lingers in our minds from three days after Easter in 1995—the bombed Alfred P. Murrah Federal Building in Oklahoma City. Our mental videos play again: a dead babe in a fireman's arms, a tiny sneaker sticking out of a heap of debris, a mother whose good-bye kiss that morning to her two lively little boys turned out to be final. And tears come. In our eyes and in our hearts. Home-grown violence made and planted a bomb, blew up innocent adults, and splashed the blood of our nation's precious babies on our national soul.

We see madness in our lack of care for our home planet. We are causing the earth's average temperature to change. Scientists believe a change in temperature of only 5° Celsius triggered the Ice Age.[2] They are predicting a temperature rise of 1° Celsius within three decades, which will raise sea levels and cause great flooding. We have shifted from thousands of years of sowing and reaping in partnership with God's good earth to stripping and raping it.

We see madness in our lack of nurturing. The family is a child's first communal experience, and that experience has become one of generationally separated families, one-parent families, changing-parent families, dual-career-centered families. This statement is not one of judgment but an observation of the incredibly difficult structures we have set up for our children and ourselves. Amitai Etzioni, author of *The Spirit of Community,* looked at the "wide variety of human societies (from the Zulus to the Inuits, from ancient

Greece and ancient China to modernity)" and found that "there has never been a society that did not have two-parent families." In *EarthCurrents*, Snyder puts forth the estimate that only two babies in ten "will be raised by both parents and grow to adulthood without experiencing parental divorce, separation, or remarriage."

We often leave the formation of our children's values to that electronic nanny whose purpose is profit. The adults surrounding a child often model placing blame rather than taking responsibility. We, of course, love our children dearly, and as parents we do the best we can in the moment. But our other priorities can leave us little time and energy for nurturing. Identity is perceived and expressed largely through relationships, like weaving our lives into a communal tapestry; but that tapestry is unraveling, and our children dangle amidst loose and fraying ends.

I do not believe we want to live this way. The popularity of the Oscar-winning movie *Forrest Gump* indicates a hunger for goodness and simplicity. The church offers a cosmic vision that transcends social madness. The writer of Ephesians prays that "according to the riches of his glory, he may grant that you may be strengthened in your inner being with power through his Spirit, and that Christ may dwell in your hearts through faith, as you are being rooted and grounded in love." As Christians in a society gone mad, God calls us to take our clay feet in a saner direction, to dare to be different—to think clearly, to be open to the power of the Spirit, and to be grounded in love.

CALLED TO COURAGE AND THE CROSS

Scripture: Mark 8:31-38

We kneel at the altar on needlepoint cushions while a hymn plays softly in the background. We look reverently toward the shiny gold cross—keeping it at a safe distance. Suddenly, the words of Jesus come to us: "If any want to become my followers, let them deny themselves and take up their cross and follow me." Whoa! *Deny* ourselves? *Take up* the cross? *Follow* Jesus' way of suffering and serving and being last instead of first? How about we just talk the talk and pay the pastor to walk the walk!

Our faith brings us comfort, but it also calls us to the cross. Jesus does not ask us to seek suffering for its own sake but to have the courage not to avoid it at all costs. The Hasidic Master Rebbe Nachman of Breslov taught, "Know! A person walks in life on a very narrow bridge. The most important thing is not to be afraid."[3] Our age has been called the age of anxiety. Fear scratches at the backdoor of our minds like scraping claws—fear of people, fear of pain, fear of aging, fear of change, fear of loss, fear of any kind of cross. Today, from the ghettos to the suburbs, we need to hear anew the words of the angel, "Do not be afraid!"

Fear divides. We live in an "anti-" time. We have trouble knowing what we're *for*, but we are clear about what we're *against*. Far more people know what they'll *kill* for than what they'll *die* for. Even the church, the reconciling body of Christ, has in some instances become a bastion of fear and divisiveness. The "left" fears the "right." The "right" fears the "left." Nouwen reminds us in *Life of the Beloved*: "Literally, the word 'diabolic' means dividing. The demon divides; the Spirit unites." Aggression and intimidation, hostility and hatred are not the way of Jesus. (But what about his Temple temper, we ask self-righteously, and all those paintings of him with whip in hand? We forget that John is the only Gospel that places a whip in the Temple story and that some versions of John restrict the whip to driving out the sheep and cattle.) The writer of Ephesians admonishes,

> Let no evil talk come out of your mouths, but only what is useful for building up, as there is need, so that your words may give grace to those who hear. . . . Put away from you all bitterness and wrath and anger and wrangling and slander, together with all malice, and be kind to one another, tenderhearted, forgiving one another, as God in Christ has forgiven you (4:29, 31-32).

Nouwen in *Life of the Beloved* says it this way: "There is no clearer way to discern the presence of God's Spirit than to identify the moments of unification, healing, restoration and reconciliation. Where the Spirit works, divisions vanish and inner as well as outer unity manifests itself."

As we wander in the wilderness, we remember once again that the Christian faith is a resurrection faith. Whereas fear condemns and polarizes, trust saves and reconciles. Whereas fear builds crosses for others to mount, trust rolls away the stones. Our faith conquers fear, both the chronic tremor scratching at the backdoor of our minds and the quaking terror of the cross. When the words of Jesus come to us to deny ourselves and take up our cross and follow him, we can trust God that beyond the cross is an opportunity for the fullness of new life. Therefore, we journey to the cross through faith, mustering our courage and lifting our heads, saying with Elie Wiesel in his novel *The Gates of the Forest*, "I'll dance anyhow."

CALLED TO BE NEW CREATURES IN CHRIST

Scripture: James 1:11-18

James tells us, "He gave us birth by the word of truth, so that we would become a kind of first fruits of his creatures." As we ponder what it means to become "a kind of first fruits," we hear the echo of Abba Anthony's words when he was asked what we must do to please God: "Whoever you may be, always have God before your eyes; whatever you do, do it according to the testimony of the holy Scriptures; in whatever place you live, do not easily leave it."[4] As new creatures in Christ we are to center our lives in God, to base our actions on the scriptures, and to be in community.

When we have God before our eyes, we see the sacred in the common. Prayers of praise and thanksgiving for all God's wonderful gifts rise in chorus with the whole community of saints who have gone before us. When we have God before our eyes, trust can overcome despair, for the transparent presence of God stands between us and our obstacles. When we have God before our eyes, we perceive our identity in relationship with God, and we become a new creature in Christ.

If whatever we do is to be done according to the scriptures, we may need to tighten up our behavior and loosen up our theology. On a beautiful Lenten day I was sitting on a park bench in Jackson Square in the French Quarter, soaking up the sunshine while writing. Someone handed me a tract. I noticed that it was about Jesus, but I didn't look up from my work because I was feeling a time crunch and didn't want to be interrupted (another Lenten confession).

"Are you saved?" he asked.

I debated ignoring him. In the first place I'm not comfortable with intrusive evangelism, and in the second place I was trying to concentrate on the writing I'd done on compassion. *Compassion.* Oops! I mustered an, "I'm saved." I don't recall ever before referring to my faith journey as being "saved."

He persisted. "Will you go to heaven when you die?"

I began to wonder if he'd read that "in-your-face evangelism" article I'd heard about. Yet he seemed like a nice young man, and he could have been spending his time doing a lot worse things—especially with Bourbon Street only two blocks away. "I'm a United Methodist."

He smiled. "That's good. My dad was a Methodist. I'm a Baptist. My pastor used to be a Methodist."

The words he and I use to talk about the faith are not the same. Neither is our approach to others regarding it. But I'm not sure these differences are relevant in God's eyes. He was spending this Lenten afternoon trying to help bring people closer to Jesus by handing out tracts and asking if they were saved. I was spending it trying to help bring people closer to the Christ by writing this book.

It seems to me that becoming "a kind of first fruits" has more to do with whether we behave according to the scriptures than how we talk about them. The New Testament makes it clear that when we choose to be selfish and greedy, immoral and unethical, power-oriented and oppressive in our Monday-to-Friday deeds and relationships, our behavior is contrary to the gospel. The seeds we plant in one season are the crop we reap the next. We cannot plant seeds of greed and reap generosity of spirit or plant seeds of corruption and reap trust. What we do at midnight is present in our heart at high noon.

Abba Anthony's words about not leaving easily from a place emphasize community. Wherever we are, we can be open to the gift of the moment—even on a park bench. Ongoing experiences of presence in the present produce more maturity in a decade than the expedience of an absent-hearted, future-oriented life plan. In *Dakota* Kathleen Norris suggests that our belief in individual accomplishment is "so strong that it favors exploitation over stewardship, mobility over stability." She reminds us that "we pay a high price for applying upward mobility to the life of the spirit, denying roots, and turning a blind eye to that which might nurture us in our own heritage." Wherever we are, our faith is communal.

Each step of the faith journey offers a gift easily missed when we are running toward the future. Instead of becoming "a kind of first fruits," James reminds us that "in the midst of a busy life, [we] will wither away."

—— ✧ ——

WE ARE CALLED TO BE NEW CREATURES in Christ, to be grounded in love and open to the breath of the Spirit moving among us personally and corporately, just as the cosmic breath moves through the pine tree outside my window. A writer described a particular community by saying that it "could not conceive a future any different from the past, could not devise innovative alternatives for tomorrow. All their knowledge, everything they did, was a repetition of something that had been done before." These words of Jean Auel, about the clan of the cave bear, are uncomfortably reminiscent of some congregations.

We are not called to repeat the past. We are called to devise faithful innovative alternatives for tomorrow. As we wander together in the wilderness, we hear the voice of John the Revelator repeat the phrase: "Listen to what the Spirit is saying to the churches" (Rev. 2:7, 11, 17, 29). It is hard to hear the Spirit amidst the chaos of today. Or perhaps that chaos itself is a message of the Spirit's urgent call to the church to be the body of Christ, recreating a sense of community and spiritual infrastructure that will offer hope and healing in the new millennium.

THOUGHTS AND REFLECTIONS

✧ Think about the Masai community described in this chapter. How is your church like that community? What differences between the two communities stand out? How can the habits and disciplines of Lent move these two communities closer together?

✧ People often make formal and informal confessions. How can confession create a deeper sense of community for you and for your church or your study group? Take time to think about your call to confession. What do we (as individuals and as a church) have to confess so that we can change?

✧ This chapter describes three conversions. Think about conversions (great and small) that you have experienced. Tell another person in your church or in your study group about one of these experiences.

✧ Have you experienced a time when you forgot compassion? What reminded you to be compassionate? When have you felt that your church's boards or councils needed reminders of compassion?

✧ How is God leading you beyond fear of old patterns and ways of doing into the newness of life in Christ?

✧ What does it mean to be a new creature in Christ? If you were to dance (as Elie Wiesel suggests) to God's new tune, what would change in your life?

✧ Consider again the question raised in chapter 1: In what direction does your spiritual compass point? For what does your soul cry? What is the essence of your life's desire? What do you most deeply yearn to do or be?

4

Words for Wanderers

$\diamond$

ords! Words! Words!" exclaims Nouwen in *The Way of the Heart*. "Over the last few decades we have been inundated by a torrent of words." In our overuse and misuse, words lose their power. For example, *awesome*—something producing "awe" ("fear mingled with admiration or reverence; a feeling produced by something majestic") is now an adjective we use to describe pizza. Yet even in this deluge of words, the Word arches over us like a rainbow. In *Gratefulness, the Heart of Prayer* Brother David Steindl-Rast says the basic biblical truth is that "'God speaks.' If God speaks, the whole universe and everything in it is word." He refers to faith as the "courage to listen." As we wander in the wilderness, let's pause for breath in our ceaseless chatter, peek at the rainbow from under an umbrella, and reflect on a few words, pondering them singly and deeply, opening ourselves to their transforming power.

PRAYER IS A Spiritual Discipline

Scripture: Psalm 32

Prayer is a fundamental spiritual discipline. Sometimes we confuse praying with saying words. But prayer is not about words. It is about transformation. Abba Macarius, a former camel-driver, was asked, "How should we pray?" He answered, "There is no need to talk much in prayer."[1] The image of the stately old "prayer" tree outside my window is a steady reminder of prayer that rises silently to God.

How should we pray? We can pray a centering prayer, a prayer with no words at all—no thoughts, no images. We simply show up at the table, presenting ourselves to God as we are.

How should we pray? We can pray through the repetition of a phrase. Or by saying a single word over and over again, focusing on it, internalizing it. (We may pray in this way with each of the word-headings in this chapter.) This repetition becomes a form of breath prayer, in which we take in the word like air and listen to what God has to tell us through it. The images that appear are, like art, opportunities for deeper meaning. The word touches our soul and becomes part of us in a new and transforming way.

How should we pray? We can pray the "Jesus Prayer," a common breath prayer that originated in the seventh century. We inhale and pray silently, *Lord Jesus Christ, Son of the Living God*; we exhale and pray silently, *Have mercy on me, a sinner*. Through that prayer we can transform our inner space regardless of our external space. We do not alter the situation itself but allow God's love, peace, and comfort to penetrate the core of our being so that the stress and pain we feel in the moment melt away, like sun melts ice. The psalmist tells us, "Therefore let all who are faithful offer prayer to you; at a time of distress, the rush of mighty waters shall not reach them."

How should we pray? In the Bible, prayer includes praise and thanksgiving, confession, forgiveness and guidance, requests for divine help and intercession. The Lord's Prayer, which Jesus taught us, is known by Christians around the world. I was struck by its universal power and mystery when I attended the World Methodist Faith Conference in Hollabrun, Austria. All of us from our many nations bowed our heads and joined reverently in that prayer, which each of us knew by heart. Its holy words filled the auditorium in seventeen different languages. Yet our voices rose and fell together with the same inflections, even the same rhythm and pauses. All of us reached the end simultaneously, proclaiming in mighty unison:

"Amen!" So be it! Through that prayer we of many countries, cultures, and languages were transformed into one body.

How should we pray? Jesus said to love our enemies and pray for those who persecute us (see Matthew 5:44). This is more than praying for God to forgive them or even that we may forgive them; it is to pray *for* them. One of the most powerful ways prayer transforms us is through the healing we receive when we pray regularly for the well-being of one who harms us. Praying sincerely for one who wreaks havoc in our lives, or did so in the past, is more difficult than radical surgery, but it makes us spiritually whole. Gradually our hearts change, and the cancer of hatred within us heals. Somehow this praying disarms others' weapons against our heart and soul. Miracle of miracles, this amazing transformation within us occurs regardless of whether the other person changes! What power there is in prayer!

How should we pray? There is no "right" way to pray. In *The Ladder of Divine Ascent* John Climacus, the most popular spiritual writer of the Orthodox Christian world since the seventh century, said, "You cannot discover from the teachings of others the beauty of prayer. Prayer has its own special teacher in God." The Teacher of Prayer does not grade our prayers, fail us or promote us, give daily assignments, restrict topics, or provide a style manual. Our task is not even to *try* to make something happen but simply to *allow* it to happen—to show up at the table (with our ears and eyes as well as our mouths).

Ann and Barry Ulanov in their article "Prayer and Personality" tell us that "prayer above all else is conversation with God. It is the primary speech of the true self to the true God." We remove our masks and to God and ourselves we reveal our false piety, our passions, our illusions. And the ever-living God of grace and love sees our unmasked face and smiles upon us.

LENTON UNMASKING

PROMISE

Scripture: John 3:14-21

Merton asks, "What am I? I am a word spoken by God."[2] My friend Frank told me about his grandmother. Through his story, she became part of my life, one of those memorable words spoken by God. I think of her as I ponder *promise*.

Buelah Akin was ninety-five years old and lived independently, served in her church and tended her garden, took care of herself and others. One day while out walking, she fell and rolled into a culvert. Her injuries were serious.

At the hospital after she had been checked over, Buelah asked, "How long before I can walk again?"

The doctor hesitated.

"*Will* I be able to walk again?"

He sighed. "It's a very serious injury."

"Please. Tell me, Doctor. *Will I ever walk again?*"

He lowered his eyes, a somber look on his face. "You can be comfortable. It will be all right."

Buelah was silent for a moment, and then she spoke calmly and firmly: "I have been on God's good earth for ninety-five years, and I have never been a burden to anyone. I don't intend to become one now." She folded her arms across her chest, closed her eyes, and spoke no more.

Two days of silence went by, and her family and the hospital staff felt sure that she was no longer lucid. In the 2 A.M. stillness of the hospital, she lay in her room alone. A nurse happened to pass by her open door and stopped just outside it. As the nurse listened, tears came to her eyes and rolled down her cheeks. Buelah Akin was praying aloud the Lord's Prayer. Clearly and distinctly, with absolute trust. Thirty minutes later, she died. The faithful word of her life was complete.

Jesus said, "For God so loved the world that he gave his only Son, so that everyone who believes in him may not perish but may have eternal life." Buelah Akin was a word spoken by God, a promise fulfilled.

POWER

Scripture: John 9

As we ponder *power*, let's look at *The Power to Bless* by Myron Madden. He discusses the impact of childhood perceptions about being the "blessed" one in a family or the one "under the curse."

When children assume that the "family, or some part of it, is hostile" toward them, one reaction is to feel they must "remain on guard lest [they] be destroyed." Another reaction is to wonder if perhaps they are adopted, for "there is frustration and a feeling of unreality and doubt about the relationship."

The child we were lingers as part of who we are as adults; for many of us that child is hungry for blessing. For example, Madden relates dependency in adulthood to the perception of being unblessed. Throughout the human family—in all cultures, colors, countries, and financial circles—there are those who perceive themselves as unblessed.

According to Madden, "Just as one life comes from another life, so blessing comes from another." Individuals who perceive themselves to be unblessed may receive transformation through awareness and acceptance of the power of God's blessing. However, Madden reminds us that an outside person "cannot intrude"; authority to heal "must be granted or permitted by the one in need, and must be asked for or sought." Becky ?!!

My Hungarian friend Andor is a blesser. He is a courageous Christian who risked crossing the border into Austria to attend a faith conference in 1988 while his country was still part of the U.S.S.R. My husband Bill and I happened to sit at Andor's table during the first meal of the conference. Bearded and stocky, Andor wore a woven woolen bag over his shoulder—explaining that this was customary in Hungary. The explanation was not easy; Andor spoke limited English, and I spoke no Hungarian. We strained to understand each other, taking the few English words he knew and making do with inflections and nods, gestures and facial expressions.

Andor's deep faith showed in his face as he told his faith story. His eyes grew intense, and I was struck by the courage and sacrifice of Hungarian Methodists who had remained faithful despite the dangers they risked under Communism. Andor's deep love for his family showed in his eyes when he spoke of them—his wife, their five children, and his mother-in-law, all of whom lived together in a three-room flat. Andor's deep care for others showed in a multitude of ways. One evening I saw him pushing a man in a wheelchair the eight blocks of pebbly rocks from the Sporthotel to the town hall for worship. His woolen bag over his shoulder as always, he entertained the man with his wonderful jokes. His robust laughter created a mood of merriment all along the way. His deep generosity showed the last day of the conference. He came up to me, holding his woolen bag, and said, "Mar-i-leen, I give you." He handed me the bag he'd worn everyday, every place he'd gone—a part of himself. It was all that he had, and he gave it away. I treasure that bag. It hangs on the wall of my little room, and I see it when I come to the table at sunrise. I look at it now and feel Andor's presence.

Andor evokes the kind of trust that invites the broken to him. Through him, as an instrument of God's healing power of blessing, they receive that long-sought gift. Andor has so little; yet, I've never known anyone who has more than he—for Andor has the power to bless.

In the Great Commission Jesus sent the disciples forth with the power of blessing. When we hear—truly hear—the message that we are beloved by God, blessed by the Holy One, that blessing can reverse any human "curse." Madden says, "The blessing is more than love—it is the very renewal of life itself." Power from the Christian perspective is about nothing less than the power to bless.

PRESENCE

Scripture: Psalm 23

How easy it is to confuse the power to bless with the power to rescue! The power to bless is a ministry of presence, not of rescue. Nouwen helps us understand the difference when he writes in *Life of the Beloved*: "I knew that the only thing I could do was to be with you, stay with you and somehow encourage you not to run away from your pain, but to trust that you had the strength to stand in it." Presence walks beside; rescue reaches down. Presence touches hearts; rescue tosses crumbs. Presence calls forth strength; rescue fosters weakness.

We see human beings at our best during heroic rescues in emergencies—like the firefighters after the bombing of the federal building in Oklahoma City. But another kind of rescue (frequently, emotional rescue) can become a subtle form of oppression. Oppression by rescue may seem like a contradiction, but let's look closely.

Though some people do have serious reasons, even medical problems, that make coping difficult, the ability to cope depends to a surprising degree on the condition of our inner lives. Friedman suggests that our capacity to cope correlates with our perception that we have the inner resources to handle the situation.[3] This bit of information helps us understand how some people astonish us with their capacity to handle incredibly difficult problems, while other people have a hard time coping with relatively minor ones. Christians are great rescuers! We mean well, but our rescue can shortcut the growth of the other's inner resources.

Rescue can foster a self-fulfilling prophecy of inadequacy, reinforcing dependency and perpetuating a victim image. Rescue can build up credit that leaves the other feeling indebted and perhaps ultimately bankrupt. Rescue can be a means to self-glorification. It can lead to a condescending attitude toward the other, so well described by Pat Conroy in *The Prince of Tides*: "Every movement he made and every word he spoke was buttery with condescension." Well-buttered, we slip away from presence.

Jesus did not rescue. Jesus healed. He healed ears to hear and eyes to see. He gave new life to the hopeless, sending them on their way to celebrate and serve. Jesus gave the gift of his presence in the present moment. To follow that example transforms our faith journey, offering us the joy of being a healing presence through the power of the Spirit.

It is very hard for us to be truly present with others in the moment—even with our loved ones. Walker Percy in *The Thanatos Syndrome* says it well: "When we're with them, we're not with them, not in the very present but casting ahead of them and the very present, planning tomorrow, regretting yesterday, worrying about money and next year." It is also hard for us to realize that in a ministry of presence, words are not important. Merton suggests that "the more words we need, the greater our poverty."

When, rich in wordlessness, we are present to others in the present, we experience a powerful joy. Among my highest moments are those spent with dear ones around the table—candlelight and flowers and beautiful music in the background (these wonderful symbols of light, life, and a universal language). In those moments at the table we offer one another the safety to unmask without fear and the sacred space to hear our own inner words of the heart rise silently to the Holy One. Around that table we feel the presence of the Spirit and an overflowing sense of healing love and mutual well-being. It is to this table that we invite one who is hurting.

As we carry our "table" of presence through the wilderness, we begin to reflect on our enemies. We recall the words of the ancient psalm: "Thou preparest a table before me in the presence of my enemies," RSV. And we also recall Jesus' teachings about our enemies. Can we prepare a table for our enemies? Can we host them? Can we be present to them? Can we be a channel of the healing Spirit even for them? Certainly not all the time—at least (another Lenten confession) I can't. But sometimes. Sometimes.

Prisoners are those whom society has declared its enemies. Kairos, a program like Cursillo or The Walk to Emmaus, is designed especially for use with those in prison. Kairos considers the *residents* (the term used by Kairos instead of *prisoners*) to be responsible for the acts that caused them to be locked away. It does not look upon them as victims, falling into the rescue trap. Instead, Kairos is a presence ministry that fosters the prisoners' development of inner resources.

I spent my last birthday in Winn Prison in Louisiana. It was a Sunday evening, and about fifty of us from various denominations gathered with the residents participating in the Kairos journey. During our time together, Bill gave each resident a cross and a hug, and each man had an opportunity to respond to his Kairos experience. A few of their remarks sketch the power of presence ministry:

> "You can't just go up to the guard and say, 'I need a hug.' But with Kairos . . ." Tears came to the eyes of this tough, six-foot-four, 250-pound man, and he couldn't finish.

> "You've got to harden your heart to make it in here. You can't get soft. But no matter how hard I tried to harden my heart this weekend, I couldn't do it."

> "Something ain't right. You're too nice to me."

"We appreciate you all for looking past our faults to see our hurts."

"Homemade cookies for me! For *me*!"

"Sometimes you need God with some flesh on."

"Most of you are professional people. And you're inside a *prison*! At *night*! With *us*!"

Some of the men mentioned the letters from children they'd received during their Kairos journey. Most of their letters came from a Catholic elementary school. One man spoke of his letter from a little girl:

"Her father died . . ." The man began to weep. "When she was two." He shook his head and struggled to regain control. "She said in her letter, 'I'll pray for you. You pray for me.'"

Another man also told of a letter from a little girl:

"She said, 'I'll pray for you for two weeks.' I keep thinking, *What's going to happen to me when the two weeks is over?*"

Before that evening I had not realized how much prisoners long for letters and how few they receive.

The warden, a large respected man with sweat rings darkening his short-sleeved shirt, spoke on this hot Louisiana November night. He said, "It takes courage even in the free world to be a Christian—but in *here*!" There was admiration in his tone as he glanced at the prisoners.

Afterward the Kairos leader gave a brief talk and explained that Kairos is not a program that comes and goes but one that stays; Kairos volunteers continue to come on a regular basis. He said that the first Kairos event was in Florida over twenty years ago, and Kairos volunteers are still present there. He offered wisdom appropriate for all of us who want to take our table to others: "Bring the word the way they need to hear it—not the way you want to tell it."

I was once on an Oklahoma jury that sent a man to prison for rape. The night of my birthday I thought of him again—as I have many times over the years. I hope someone is present to him, someone to give him a kind word and a chaste hug.

PERCEPTION

Scripture: 2 Corinthians 5:16-21

Marius von Senden in *Space and Flight* tells about a young blind girl whose father longs for her to receive sight. Finally an operation succeeds. How her father rejoices! At last his daughter can see! But later, he watches sadly as she walks through the familiar rooms of her house with her eyes closed. Perhaps God rejoices that though once we were blind now we can see, yet watches us sadly as we walk through the familiar rooms of the faith with our eyes closed, comfortable with our old perceptions of reality.

Walking with our eyes closed, we tend to categorize groups of people (by faith, geographic region, age, race, political party) and be done with them. Rebbe Nachman in *The Empty Chair* warns, "Even with a good eye, be careful not to rush judgment. This is no different than looking at something from afar and drawing the wrong conclusion." Even if we do draw close, we find it difficult to dispel our preconceived (prejudged or prejudiced) images.

Oklahoma State University conducted a study to determine whether close positive contact could change children's negative images of elderly persons. The results were surprising. The children's perception of the specific persons with whom they were involved *did* change; their negative image of elderly people as a group did *not* change. Instead, the children simply decided that their new friends were not old! When we apply this study to broader human relations, we realize that even though stereotyped categories are unlikely to change, one-to-one relationships do change images of individuals. One-to-one. But of course! Isn't that how we invite people to our table?

Walking with our eyes closed, we tend to ignore our cultural blindness. In an article "Seeing with a Native Eye," Barre Toelken suggests that we see with the "native eye"—we see what our culture "has trained us to see." Therefore, different groups of people "'see' things in different ways." Generally in our country, lines are prominent: straight rows of plantings to control nature, boundary fences to divide property, hierarchical ladders, relational triangles. Even most tables are rectangular with a head and a foot. However, circles are prominent images in many Native American traditions, whose

Knights of The Round Table!!

spirituality honors round Mother Earth and round Father Sun. Traditionally the people sit in circles, dance in circles, and celebrate the circle of the seasons. Circles. But of course! ~~For faith is a circle, a circle of love, inclusive and ever-widening.~~ *Very insightful*

Walking with our eyes closed, we see ~~what~~ we believe. We don't have to open our eyes because we're already sure what's there. We tend to remember experiences that support our beliefs and unconsciously dismiss or reinterpret experiences that refute them. Says Marceline in Andre Gide's *The Immoralist*: "Don't you realize that our own eyes magnify and exaggerate whatever they happen to see—that we make anyone become what we claim he is?" Everyday, ~~growing up in the past~~ and ~~going about our business in the present~~, our family, schoolmates, neighborhood, congregation, social group, and work colleagues have reinforced our ~~subcultural blindness~~. Maybe we believe that people are bad, and therefore that is what we see. Or maybe we believe that government officials ~~are going~~ to get us, and therefore that is what we see. Or we may believe that all persons from a region different from our own or from an ethnic or racial background that differs from ours ~~can't be trusted~~. And contempt, anger, and hatred grow. But if we open our newly sighted eyes, what we see astounds us. We see the face of Christ in the other—even in *that* one. But of course! "From now on, therefore, we regard no one from a human point of view."

Toelken says, "Before we can see, we must learn how to look." This struggle is not new. In ancient times. a judge went looking for Abba Moses and returned disappointed, complaining that all he saw was "an old man, tall and dark, wearing the oldest possible clothes." And he was told, "That was Abba Moses."[4] The judge did not know how to look beyond his assumptions. During our wilderness journey, we open our eyes to examine our assumptions and beliefs. We try to learn how to look ~~through Jesus' eyes~~, and our perceptions change. Like seeing for the first time, we gain an amazing new vision of God's world: "So if anyone is in Christ, there is a new creation: everything old has passed away; see, everything has become new!"

PROCLAMATION

Scripture: Ephesians 5:6-14

As we ponder *proclamation*, we tend to think of Sunday sermons. Regardless of pastors' meetings and responsibilities and crises of the week, regardless of tensions within their family, regardless of whether their personal faith journey is descending into the valley or ascending toward the mountaintop—come Sunday morning pastors have the sacred responsibility to proclaim the word of God. The preacher stands before a congregation that is diverse in age, theology, material wealth, political views, and core values. One worshiper is mature in the faith, another is a spiritual toddler. One is contemplating marriage, another divorce. One is about to bring new life into the world, another is on the verge of suicide. One has just "struck gold" in some form, another faces outer or inner bankruptcy.

The preacher looks out over the congregation and surely prays from the heart to speak words that will witness to the Word in some way to each of these people. And many of us who sit in the pews experience the worship service as a mini-journey of self-examination and spiritual renewal. We sit on the edge of our pew and listen intently for the word of God to come personally to us through the words of the preacher.

However, not all of us view the sermon so loftily. John Updike wittily depicts one view of preaching in *The Witches of Eastwick*. Two characters discuss Brenda, recently separated from her clergy husband Ed who has skipped town:

> "[They] have encouraged her to put in for Ed's position at the church and become the new Unitarian minister. . . ."
>
> "But she's not ordained. . . ."
>
> "No, but she *is* in the parsonage . . . and making her the new minister might be more graceful than getting her to leave. . . ."
>
> "But can she preach? You *do* have to preach."
>
> "Oh, I don't think that would be any real problem. Brenda has wonderful posture."

Some of us in the congregation check the preacher's posture and then doze off to sleep. Others of us pray for a short message so we can get to the restaurant ahead of the crowd. And a few of us listen intently for grammatical errors. Clergy square their shoulders before the congregation, recognizing that in the eyes of some worshipers posture is more important than homily. Wondering if *this* is the time about which Second Timothy warned, "For the time will come when they will not stand wholesome teaching, but will follow their own fancy and gather a crowd of teachers to tickle their ears" (4:3, NEB), some clergy—understandably but unfaithfully—begin to tickle our ears. Instead of preaching the awakening word of God, they tell a bedtime story. Or they exchange the Word for comfortable clichés that promote a good-luck-charm religion. Or they reduce the Word to one-phrase repetitive chants that anesthetize listeners into feeling great without thinking straight. Or they translate the word of God into expedient double-talk so that honest transvaluation of the scriptures hides in ambiguity. And as the clergy tickle our ears, perhaps vainglory raises its ugly head within them.

Proclamation is much broader than the clergy's Sunday morning sermons. Proclamation is the day-to-day, year-by-year, ongoing sermons preached in the world by our *lives*—whether clergy or lay. I think of the slice of the world on Canal Boulevard in New Orleans. Noise abounds. Cabs honk. Tourists laugh. Taped music emerges from the open doors of the stores. Jazz sets the beat from Bourbon Street. And at the intersection where St. Charles on the north side of Canal meets Rue Royale on the south side stand the street preachers, megaphone to mouth, shouting above the bedlam. That style of witness is not one many of us would choose. Yet as Christians we are street preachers; our silent life-sermons proclaim the gospel in the church meeting, the home, the workplace—and even when we walk down the street.

Our life is a series of sermons—some faithful, some not so faithful. They reveal our journey toward maturity (or "perfection," as John Wesley called it). In *The Practice of the Presence of God* Brother Lawrence, a French laybrother, ponders whether he has used his years to love and to serve God: "I am filled with shame and embarrassment when I reflect, on the one hand, on the great graces which God has granted me and which [God] continues without surcease to grant me and, on the other hand, how poorly I have used them and how little I have profited from them on the way to perfection." As we examine our own faith journey, we can only say, "Amen."

The word *preach* contains *reach* and also *each*. For me, that is a reminder not only to the pastor on Sunday morning but also to us in our silent life-sermons. Thomas Merton wrote in his journal, "This morning, before speaking, I felt very strongly the limitations imposed on me by my absurd desire to speak well . . . . Instead of simply desiring to speak as best I could in order to please God." Merton provides simple and profound insight about faithful proclamation: It is to be the best that can be done, and its purpose is to please God not elevate self. We *reach* toward *each* one we encounter in the best way we can in the moment, motivated by pleasing God, not elevating self. That subtle shift transforms our lives. We preach faithfully when we "live as children of light—for the fruit of the light is found in all that is good and right and true."

PASCHA

Scripture: Psalm 22

The celebration of the *Pascha*—the passion (suffering and death) and resurrection of the Lord—is the church's oldest liturgical observance. The Paschal (sometimes spelled *pascal*) baptism was the time the early church received persons "of real sincerity in their Christian profession" after six weeks of instruction, preparation, and times of fasting. The Paschal vigil, held on the Saturday night and Sunday morning of Easter, stems from the weekend vigil of New Testament times.

The Paschal candle is a large candle on its own stand that is lit during the vigil. Its fire and light symbolize the triumph of the Resurrection over darkness and sin. By the end of the fourth century, the Paschal celebration included light, word, water, and the bread and wine of the Eucharist. (We realize how precious those elements were in that day—for there was no light switch as they walked into a room; no bombardment of words from junk mail, television, and the Internet; no water faucet at the kitchen sink; no knob to adjust the oven heat.) These elements were "symbols conveying the power of the redeeming Christ to the gathered assembly." The Paschal celebration did not merely recall past events but brought their power to worshipers, who made a renewed encounter with the Lord. *Paschal* is also a term pertaining to Passover and applied to the lamb slaughtered for the Passover feast, which explains the image of Jesus as the sacrificial lamb.

As we pray the word *pascha* in a breath prayer, repeating it, focusing on it, turning it over in our minds and hearts, we force ourselves to encounter the suffering Jesus. We do not want to think about our Lord's physical suffering as the sacrificial lamb. The image of the Christmas babe in the manger brings a smile to our lips and joy to our hearts, but we shove the horror of the suffering Christ at Golgotha from our minds—the blood-streaked, beaten Jesus hanging from the cross, the crown of twisted thorns, the spit of the soldiers on his face, the nail holes in his hands. (I can hardly bear to write these words.) The Gospel of Mark tells us: "At three o'clock Jesus cried out with a loud voice, '*Eloi, Eloi, lema sabachthani?*' which means, 'My God, my God, why have you forsaken me?'" (Mark 15:33). Many scholars believe that these words from the cross were not a cry that meant Jesus felt forsaken by God, but that he was beginning to recite Psalm 22, for the ancient words match his last hours:

> My God, my God, why have you forsaken me? . . . Do not be far from me, for trouble is near and there is no one to help. . . . I am poured out like water, and all my bones are out of joint. . . . My mouth is dried up like a potsherd. . . . A company of evildoers encircles me. . . . They stare and gloat over me. . . . They divide my clothes among themselves, and for my clothing they cast lots. . . . Deliver my soul from the sword.[5]

Then the psalm moves into praise:

> He did not hide his face from me, but heard when I cried to him. . . . Those who seek him shall praise the Lord. . . . All the ends of the earth shall remember and turn to the Lord. . . . And I shall live for him. . . . Future generations will be told about the Lord, and proclaim his deliverance to a people yet unborn.[6]

The psalm was familiar to the Jewish people watching at Golgotha, and they would have known that it moved from pain to praise.

Jesus puts not only our faith but also our suffering in a new perspective. An important dimension of the Lenten pilgrimage is to face our mortality. It is also important to accept the pain in our lives fully rather than denying it, thereby opening ourselves to God's transformational power through our suffering.

My friend Nancy Miller comes vividly to mind. She lived out her faith, discovering her gifts and giving them away. Her small space on the planet was filled with flowers, for wherever she walked her special touch helped others blossom. Nancy arose one morning, thanked God for the day, got her children off to school, and kept her appointment to see the doctor—an appointment that ended in a diagnosis of acute leukemia and a maximum of three years to live. Nancy was thirty-three; her children were five, seven, and nine. *Why couldn't life come to her as she had dreamed and deserved!*

As Nancy carried this cross, she knew moments of doubting God, surges of anger, days of depression. But the light of love inevitably followed the darkness of despair. She walked forward on the faith journey one step at a time—thanking God every morning with a special sense of gratitude for each new day, nurturing her garden of relationships, saying no to death.

Over time, the drugs fighting the disease took their toll. She developed emphysema. A book lover, her vision faded and finally, even with the thickest glasses, she was unable to read. But she continued to nurture those around her, calling them into bloom.

One January weekend she mustered all the strength left in her ninety remaining pounds. Wheezing and coughing, putting drops in her eyes every few minutes, she led a youth retreat. With a frail hand and a powerful faith, she touched the lives of those young people in a way they will always remember. She reflected the love of Christ. She showed them gratitude for the earth and its family and each new sunrise. Her faith shone on them, and their petals unfolded.

With the coming spring, Nancy began to speak of being tired for the first time. Her *youngest* child was now ready to graduate from high school and had been accepted at the college of his choice. Nancy—having broken all medical records for her type of leukemia—went to the hospital for the final time. No longer able to tend her garden of relationships, she at last said yes to death—*twelve years* after her diagnosis. Twelve years of suffering, growing, and giving herself away in a celebration of life—whatever its terms.

Brother Lawrence wrote the final letter of his life a week before he died in 1691: "If our love of God is great, we will love Him equally in sorrow and in joy." Nancy did not write a letter, but I see her love of God in the beautiful garden she left behind, colorful flowers scattered all across Oklahoma where the pathway of her life touched others. At Golgotha, Jesus showed us how to suffer and ultimately how to die. The way we deal with our suffering is one of the most faithful sermons our lives can preach.

= ✧ =

"IN THE BEGINNING WAS THE WORD, and the Word was with God, and the Word was God" (John 1:1). Second Timothy warns, "Avoid profane chatter, for it will lead people into more and more impiety, and their talk will spread like gangrene" (2:16-17). Our own words fall somewhere between the Holy Word and profane chatter. They can be weapons or windows or wisdom. They signal what is in our hearts.

THOUGHTS AND REFLECTIONS
✧

- ✧ What does it mean to be present to another? When have you experienced the full presence of another?
- ✧ Think about the section on perception. What groups of people do you *categorize* rather than see? What groups does the church pigeonhole? Why do we resist changing our perceptions?
- ✧ How do you understand the partnership between pew and pulpit? How do you expect to receive the word of God in worship? On what factors does hearing the word of God in a sermon depend?
- ✧ Think about the symbols used in the Paschal vigil: light, word, water, bread and wine. Contemplate each symbol as you remember the passion and resurrection of Jesus Christ. How do these symbols remind us of Jesus' commitment to face suffering and continue to serve God?
- ✧ Try this activity based on the different parts of speech. If each of us is a word spoken by God, what kind of word do you think you most often are in the sentence of the church? (Remember that a noun may be a subject or an object; a verb is active or passive, past, present, or future tense; an adjective describes another word and may be in the shadow of the other; an adverb modifies the behavior of another; the conjunction connects different thoughts.)

5

TRUST HEALS HEARS
FEAR HURTS HATES
GIVES
TAKES

Witnessing to the Wonder

he wonder! The Christ. The cross. The creation of a new
way. A way that leaps beyond logic. A way that ~~trusts~~
instead of fears. A way that ~~heals~~ instead of hurts. A
way that ~~hears~~ instead of hates. A way that ~~gives~~ instead
of takes. In *The Sacred Journey* Frederick Buechner
says, "Above all, never question the truth beyond all understanding
and surpassing all other wonders that in the long run nothing, not
even the world, not even ourselves, can separate us forever from that
last and deepest love that glimmers in our dusk like a pearl, like a
face." The wonder! In the name of Jesus Christ we witness to the
wonder of that love.

REMEMBERING OUR BAPTISM

Scripture: Jeremiah 31:31-34

As we wander in the wilderness, we reflect upon our own baptismal
journey. Historically this reflection is part of the Lenten pilgrimage.
Baptism is not static but dynamic. Our "baptism is permanent," says
James White in *Sacraments as God's Self Giving.* "But renewal of it
is a lifelong process." We *are*, not *were*, baptized. Do we remember
our baptism?

The most recent of my family members to be baptized was my grandson Nathan. We gathered around him at the church—his parents, grandparents, aunts, uncles, and young cousins Chelsea and Sarah. As we stood at the chancel, Nathan's grandfather, his aunt, and the pastor administered the sacrament of baptism. Then the pastor carried Nathan down the long center aisle while the congregation offered words of litany and song, welcoming him into the church family. As the pastor neared the sanctuary door, little Chelsea leaned against me and whispered in alarm, "Grandmom! Is the minister taking Nathan *out*?"

I whispered the truth, "No. It's all right." But the *truth* is "yes." Our baptism takes us *out*.

Our baptism (or confirmation of the vows made on our behalf in infancy) takes us *out* into a new way of being in the world. A single drop of water in Christian baptism has more power than all the ocean waves combined. With that droplet of water, symbolically the old self dies and the new self begins to emerge. Grace greets guilt and trust meets anxiety. We walk forward in the Spirit on the path of Christ. Baptism is the first step in a lifelong journey of returning to God with all our heart. Do we remember our baptism?

Our baptism takes us *out* into ministry. Whether clergy or laity, baptism calls us to ministry in the name of Jesus Christ. White says that baptism unites us not only "to Jesus Christ himself but to all he does. Christ's work is made ours. . . . Baptism is the foundation of the ministry or priesthood of all Christians." Baptism introduces us to servanthood and sacrifice, thereby introducing us to life. In the giving of ourselves, full life comes to us. Do we remember our baptism?

Our baptism takes us *out* into a new covenant, a sacred unity of creature with creation and Creator. In Jeremiah we read, "I will put my law within them, and I will write it on their hearts; and I will be their God, and they shall be my people." Our new covenant, written on our hearts, does not change God; it changes our innermost being. In *The Woman at Otowi Crossing*, Frank Waters says, "Each cell, each atom and solar system repeated in its constant movement the same great in-breathing and out-breathing rhythm of the whole, the pulse of life itself." It is the Creator of that pulse, of that great in-breathing and out-breathing, with whom we have a new covenant.

It is to the rhythm of that pulse and with that breath that, remembering our baptism, we dance with the Creator!

REMEMBERING OUR NAME

Scripture: Psalm 126

My friend Mona did a door-to-door campaign when she ran for public office. On a sweltering July afternoon of 110°, she hurried up the steps of a crumbling cement porch and knocked. Finally a face peeked from behind the lace curtain and the door opened a crack. An elderly woman stood before Mona, her eyes blank. A brown chenille robe hung open over her black dress, and a yellow straw hat with a plastic iris topped her gray hair. Long red beads adorned her neck, and fuzzy green slippers hid her feet. Concerned by the woman's appearance, Mona asked, "What is your name?" The woman paused, wiped her hand across the dots of perspiration on her brow, and stammered softly, "I . . . I don't remember." Do we remember our name?

The biblical world linked name closely to personality. Before the Exile, parents gave a child a particular name because of its intrinsic significance. Frequently the name represented a circumstance at birth: Rachel, dying in childbirth, named her son Ben-oni ("son of my sorrow"). Sometimes the name signified the parents' gratitude: Judah ("praised") or reflected their aspirations for the child: Obadiah ("servant of Yahweh"). At times the name indicated a personal characteristic of the child: Esau ("hairy"). A change of name could reflect a change in character or status: Simon to Peter, Saul to Paul. After 5 B.C., we find children named after a relative or historically distinguished person. Throughout the Bible, the naming of children was important; their essence was concentrated in their name.

Do we remember our name? It is Sunday morning. The congregation has gathered. Parents present an infant for baptism, and we listen to the familiar ritual: *What name is given this child?* Perhaps parents choose a biblical name. Or they borrow a historical name, or pass down family names. Or they invent an original name or combine favorite persons' names into a new name. Perhaps they choose a month, a gem, or a flower.

Most of us go through life called by a *given* name not a *chosen one.* Nevertheless, that name forms an image of us in others' minds and shapes us to some degree. Our name reveals our parents' tastes and priorities at the time of our birth. I think of the man who ordained my husband, a man born with the surname Lord and given the name John Wesley. What could a John Wesley Lord do with his life but become a United Methodist bishop! There is power in giving a name.

There is also power in withholding a name. In *Parting the Waters* Taylor Branch reminds us that one of the psychologically destructive forces of slavery was the lack of claim to the birthright of one's name: *Maintain Superiority-Control*

> Under slavery, a name was the property of the master and not of the slave, so that a slave's name frequently changed at the auction block and sometimes on the whim of the master. Among the joyous feelings most frequently mentioned by freed or escaped slaves was the freedom to choose a name.

What name is given this child? In the Russian Orthodox tradition, the naming of a child is so sacred that the parents do not reveal the chosen name prior to the baptism. That hallowed, powerful moment of baptism is the first time anyone speaks the child's Christian name aloud.

Do we remember our name? Ralph Ellison wrote that "it is through our names that we first place ourselves in the world."[1] Today, as in biblical times, sometimes a life change is so significant, either in essence or perception, that persons mark it by a change in name. When the white smoke rises over the Vatican, the elected pope selects a new name. In 1934, the Reverend M. L. King, Sr., took a long trip abroad and chose to commemorate the significance of his journey by changing his first name from Michael to the historic Martin. For consistency he also changed the name of his five-year-old son. The boy's new name, with the expectations of its tradition, made an irreversible and continuing impact on the life of Martin Luther King, Jr.

Do we remember our name? According to Joseph Campbell in *Myths to Live By*, we project masks "upon others spontaneously, which obscure them, and to which we then react." Certain positions take on mythological status, and people respond not to the individual personality but to the mythological role. These positions eclipse the person, for the associated personage is so strong that the title can stand alone: Reverend, Doctor, Judge, Senator, Bishop, General. Perhaps we give some of these title-bearers respect without knowing them as individuals and simply expect them to be worthy and to have integrity, to demonstrate principles, ethics, and moral codes.

Or perhaps we automatically resent them, even hate them. C. G. Jung speaks of a "*mana-personality*," one charged with the magic of an imposing social mask.[2] When human weakness rips away the mask and taints the title, perhaps we feel that we have lost something in our own lives, and that loss breeds general distrust of everyone who holds that position or title. Or perhaps we receive reinforcement of our categorical resentment and hatred.

Some of us are title-bearers ourselves. Whether we wish it or not, we find a mask thrust upon us. How easy it is to allow that mask to become a permanent disguise, to sell our soul to the title, to develop an insatiable hunger for self-importance, to begin to misuse the power of the mythological role, and to find ourselves sucked into the quicksand of our own megalomania.

Do we remember our name? We are baptized with a Christian name—it is in Christ that we have our identity. And it is through Christ that we know the Source of our identity. In Isaiah we read, "It is I, the Lord, the God of Israel, who call you by your name" (45:3). We have all experienced those rare moments when we feel in tune with a divine plan and energized by a guiding force directed by God. We sense a synergetic wholeness (holiness), for we are more than we are. We are bigger than ourselves. We rise to the occasion. We are fulfilled. Our cup runneth over. Whatever words we choose to describe it, in those moments a transformation occurs. That addedness, that consciousness, that energy, that transformation is the phenomenon of hearing God call us by name.

We cannot sustain those moments of spiritual clarity. But those moments can sustain us. They sustain us even when we—like the disheveled old woman who opened the door to my friend Mona—forget our name and stand before God in a misfitting costume of a surrogate self. The moments of spiritual clarity sustain us until God loves us out of our amnesia, and once again we remember our name. It is as though we "go out weeping, bearing the seed for sowing"; and when we hear God call us by name, we "come home with shouts of joy, carrying [our] sheaves," witnessing to the wonder.

REARRANGING AND CHANGING

Scripture: Psalm 116:1-9

For 2,000 years clergy and laity have spoken many eloquent and fiery words of witness: words about redeeming the world, about marching forth into mission and witnessing to the wonder—only to trip over relational dynamics before reaching the door. (Paul's letters confirm that this problem is not a new one!) After all, we "walk before the Lord in the land of the living"—not in the land of the perfected.

As church families at our best, we facilitate one another's growth toward becoming mature persons in Christ. At our worst, the young (immature) parts of us surface, and we try to guilt-trip, manipulate, and polarize others. Friedman's work (*Generation to Generation*) helps us understand both the negative and positive dynamics in the congregational family. Applying family systems theory to the church, he speaks of a "triangle of families": the clergy family, the congregation itself, and the family units within the congregation. Though each component in the triangle is distinct, their emotional forces interlock, and "unresolved issues in any one of them can produce symptoms in the others." The positive aspects of each of the families in the triangle also spill over into the others, for "increased understanding of any one creates more effective functioning in all three."

What goes on, positively or negatively, in the parsonage family ripples into the congregation; what goes on in the congregational family affects the parsonage. Therefore, a parsonage family that is relatively healthy in its relational patterns can help lead the congregation toward maturity; just as a relatively healthy congregation can help move the parsonage family toward maturity. Likewise, the family units in the congregation affect the congregation as a whole—just as the congregation as a whole affects its family units.

We know all this, of course. It's common sense. But we don't think about its effect on our witness as a church.

Assumptions and expectations further complicate relations within the congregation. We dance toward or away from one another depending on our impressions (whether experiential, image-bound, or drawn from gossip). Hearing through our own mind-set, we tend to reinforce our own assumptions and expectations by the way we interpret what the other says. For example, if we have favorable thoughts and feelings about another, we tend to hear positively what he or she says like, "I missed you in church on Sunday." We believe the person is being kind. We feel missed, and we respond to the comment warmly—with our words, facial expression, and body language. The other sees and hears our warmth, which feels good and evokes a warm response in return. And we continue together in a happy dance.

However, if we have unfavorable thoughts and feelings about the other, the reverse happens. We hear differently whatever is said—even if it is the very same thing: "I missed you in church on Sunday." We think the person is being critical of our absence. We feel discounted, and we respond accordingly. The other person notes our distancing, which doesn't feel good to him or her, and this evokes a similarly further distancing response. And we dance away from each other with our assumptions and expectations reinforced, our separation ever-widening.

Albert Ellis, the father of Rational Emotive Therapy (RET), puts it as simply as A-B-C.[3] When A (an Action or event) happens, our B (Belief or interpretation) regarding that action determines the C (Consequences upon us—how we feel about it). We have a choice at point B, for others' actions have alternative interpretations. We can choose from among them, rearranging our thoughts and interpretations and changing our response accordingly. In building relationships, especially in the church family, it helps to pause and think about how we are interpreting another's action and to realize that other options are possible.

Going beyond the work of Ellis, I would like to add D-E-F. Just as how we interpret another's action toward us affects our feelings, our feelings affect D (what we Do)—the words and behaviors with which we respond. What we do becomes the other's E (Event or action)—which takes us full circle to *A-B-C* for the other person. And the cycle repeats itself. And the relationship whirls in a positive or negative direction. To bring in *F* (Faith) is to ask ourselves if our interpretations of what others say and do are in keeping with the teachings of our faith. In *Soul Making* Alan Jones speaks of the importance of "looking" and defines it as "a contemplative willingness to see what is there in front of us without prematurely interpreting what we see." We can choose to look and to listen through the eyes and ears of faith, increasing our repertoire of responses to others and trusting grace when we fall short.

Witnessing in today's world calls for changed ways of being together within the congregation and for fearless ways of ministering beyond its walls. It is time to pick ourselves up in our relationships and get out the door. David Bosch in *Transforming Mission* writes, "Incorporation into the Christ-event moves the individual believer into the community of believers. The church is the place where [we] celebrate [our] new life in the present and stretch out to what is still to come." The church is the place where we celebrate together and s-t-r-e-t-c-h spiritually, mentally, and relationally so that we can witness in a way that transforms this new world into God's holy community.

RE-VIEWING THE MINISTRY OF THE LAITY

Scripture: Philippians 3:4-14

We were called at our baptism to share in the ministry of Jesus Christ. Bosch goes on to say that in the New Testament "the Spirit . . . has been given to the whole people of God, not to select individuals," and the "priesthood of the ordained ministry is to enable, not to remove, the priesthood of the whole church." As baptized Christians, our vocation is ministry. In *Ministry and Solitude* James Fenhagen suggests that "ministry is not primarily an activity, but the fundamental expression of one's life in Christ." He adds, "Vocation is rooted in prayer. It is the response with our lives to what we discern as God's purpose for us."

A few years ago I was one of the speakers at a visioning conference of church leaders—primarily clergy. As they dreamed of the future, they looked at our struggling world and longed for the presence of the church in every place of need: for example, in hospitals, education, environment, peace and justice. Like many well-meaning church leaders, they forgot that the church is *already* present—in all of those areas—through the laity in the workplace. We already have a church presence through laypersons in every hospital—doctors, nurses, dietitians. We already have laypersons in education—teachers, principals, custodians, and other staff. We are already on college campuses—in teaching, administration, security, maintenance. We are working with water projects and energy research. We are in peace and justice—clerks, bailiffs, judges. We are wardens and prison guards. We are in business, marketing, and factories. We are in retail and wholesale businesses. We are in hospice, literacy, and shelter programs. We are assisting with migrant needs—indeed, we are also among the migrant workers. We are *already* out there! But most of us are not *sent!*

Serving within the walls of the church is an important part of lay ministry. However, it is only a part. The ministry of the laity is not to be "mini-pastors," but according to Jurgen Moltmann, this ministry is offered "in shops, villages, farms, cities, classrooms, homes, law offices, in counselling, politics, statecraft, and recreation."[4] Thomas Berry in *The Dream of the Earth* concurs, for "the ultimate spiritual issues are those dealt with in the cruel and compassionate world of active human existence, in the marketplace, in the halls of justice and injustice, in the places where the populace lives and works and suffers and dies." Our ministry as laypersons extends to our workplace. Every job—whatever it is—can be an arena for ministry. This understanding gives new meaning to our work. It is as though our job, small as it may be in the eyes of the world, is consecrated in the eyes of God.

John B. Cobb, Jr., in *Lay Theology* writes,

> At some times and places the church has recognized the need to help lay people think about their workaday lives from a Christian point of view. Especially in West Germany after World War II lay academies flourished. Factory workers met to reflect as Christians about their work as laborers. Business people, lawyers, doctors, and teachers also did so.

However, the ministry of the laity in the workplace is rarely viewed—by clergy or laity—as an extension of the church's ministry. Congregational leaders seldom *send* laity out as disciples to walk through the day in their workplace in a way that witnesses to God's love and grace—not by preaching but by modeling, by reflecting the spirit of Jesus Christ. Bosch tells us the church "is that community of people who are involved in creating new relationships among themselves and in society at large and, in doing this, bearing witness to the lordship of Christ." He summarizes Paul's admonitions that believers be different from others

> by abstaining from every form of evil (1 Thes 5:22), by giving offense to nobody (1 Cor 10:32), by being 'blameless and innocent, children of God without blemish in the midst of a crooked and perverse generation' (Phil 2:15), and by filling their thoughts with all that is true, honorable, just, pure, lovely, and gracious (Phil 4:8).

Paul is not talking about ethics and knowing what is good; he is talking about faith and knowing who is Lord.

Living under Christ's lordship is not easy, especially in some workplaces. As laity, we need the rhythm of going out to serve and returning to the congregation for renewal:

> GO! Go to serve faithfully in your ministry in your work place—to be the "face of Christ" in that place and to see the face of Christ in those you serve. KNOW! Know that whatever your work, however "menial," it is significant as ministry. And COME! Come when you are empty and weary, discouraged and bruised. Come for worship and renewal, en*courage*ment and a sense of belonging.

The church of vision will provide this rhythm, empowering us as laity, equipping and supporting us for our ministries beyond its walls, *sending* us out to dance in the workplace. This is not the way it has been, but it is the way it could be; for "this one thing [we] do: forgetting what lies behind and straining forward to what lies ahead."

In his book *Wishful Thinking* Frederick Buechner defines vocation as "the place where your deep gladness and the world's deep hunger meet." I believe that laypersons—empowered by the church, living out our lives where our deep gladness touches the world's deep need, being intentional about our ministry to others as we do our jobs around the world—have the combined potential to transform the planet earth into the holy community of God.

RE-CREATING SPIRITUAL LEADERSHIP

Scripture: Isaiah 43:16-21

A. Bartlett Giamatti, a past president of Yale University, defined leadership as "the assertion of a vision." Spiritual leadership is spiritual vision, a sacred seeing. This vision is not just a paint-by-number copy of what has been in the past. Isaiah speaks the Lord's word afresh to us: "I am about to do a new thing; now it springs forth, do you not perceive it?" Spiritual leadership (clergy and lay) plants its roots in the sacred and reaches toward the vision of God's ever-emerging "new thing."

Over many years of working with families, churches, and secular organizations, Friedman has concluded that the health of any group correlates with the leader's capacity "to take well-defined stands, to remain connected, to work on vision."[5] A story about Mahatma Gandhi demonstrates this kind of leadership. At a banquet a few years back I had the privilege of sitting at the table with Gandhi's grandson. He told how the big stack of mail would arrive—his hands measuring a space a foot high—and each envelope would be opened carefully because his grandfather wrote on the backs of the letters and reused the envelopes. Recounting a childhood memory, he told this story:

> Once when I was a little boy, I threw away a short pencil. When I went to my grandfather to ask for another, he told me to find the pencil and bring it to him for his own judgment. I got a flashlight and searched for almost two hours in the darkness. Finally, I found it. I felt sure that when my grandfather saw it—for it was only about three inches long—he would agree that I needed another.
>
> When I returned to him, he looked at the pencil and said, "Come sit beside me." Then he began to tell me how much of

nature is in a pencil and how hard people work to make one. He told me how many people in the world do not have pencils and paper, and how the waste of the privileged makes it harder for the others.

I did not get a new pencil.

This story demonstrates the strength of leadership of the *Mahatma* (Great Soul). His strong identity and clear values allowed him to take well-defined stands. He remained connected with those he led—"Come sit beside me." He had a vision of partnership with all human beings and all of creation, appreciating *everything*—no matter how small—as a gift of the earth. Spiritual vision remains a fantasy if we lack the strength of identity to step toward that vision and to lead others to its implementation.

It is an illusion that a person can be a leader without self-differentiation—"the capacity to be an 'I' while remaining connected" (*Generation to Generation*). This has to do with identity, with remembering our name. It is also an illusion that a person can be a *spiritual* leader without spirituality. The Christian faith incorporates but transcends do-good activities that, though vital, can become like a forest of many trees in which we lose our direction.

Our Christian heritage does not affirm spirituality without action; neither does it affirm action without spirituality. Ours is a piety of *spirituality for action*. It is the dimension of spirituality—of the heart and church and Bible, of solitude and faith and study, of social holiness—that gives us direction. Without the dimension of spirituality, we simply reflect the culture around us; we do not *creatively*—resourced by the Creator—reshape the culture.

Effective visionary spiritual leadership of both clergy and laity is vital today. This kind of leadership can move a congregation toward holy moments and sacred seeing. Strengthened through life in the Spirit, the congregation can be transformed into a revitalized community of faith that is, by its very being, a witness to the wonder. And these empowered and faithful communities can dance through the streets of the world, bringing the light of God's "new thing" into the darkness.

REANOINTING OUR LORD

Scripture: John 12:1-8

One of the major ways we witness is through our hospitality. In his book *Reaching Out* Nouwen reminds us that in the biblical sense, hospitality is to offer the gift of oneself to others, to be receptive and creatively responsive to their gifts, "to bring new life to each other." This hospitality is the kind we see in Mary's anointing of Jesus at Bethany. Anointing was a way of investing someone with power, perhaps signifying divine sanctification and approval. Hebrew Scriptures refer to the king as "the Lord's anointed" (1 Samuel 24:6), later becoming the Hebrew term *mashiah* (Messiah) and the Greek term *christos* (Christ). In the ancient Near East, anointing with aromatic oils was a sign of luxury or festivity.

When Mary anointed Jesus with the perfume of nard, Judas asked, "'Why was this perfume not sold for three hundred denarii and the money given to the poor?' (He said this not because he cared about the poor, but because he was a thief)." And Jesus' response showed that he saw through the question to its source. How often persons and congregations ask that same question in various ways! We mean well but, like Judas, we are thieves. *Ouch* !!

Judas's words stole from "the poor." He limited their repertoire of responses. He spoke *for* them, not *with* them, deciding—without consultation—that they would want that money for themselves instead of sharing symbolically in the anointing of Jesus, the Messiah, the Christ. Judas's accusation was a confession of his own stingy soul. He was not offering "the poor" the hospitality of his heart but using them for his own pompous self-righteousness. Judas was the "poor" one, for he did not know how to offer the gift of himself to others.

One of my treasured memories is being in Varna, Bulgaria, when the Reverend Zdravko Beslov received the 1992 World Methodist Peace Award. His physical condition showed the beatings and persecution he had suffered while imprisoned for his faith when Bulgaria was under Communism. But Christ was his Lord—prior to Communist rule, during his years in the prison camp, and in the free world once again. In his abundant gratitude, Pastor Beslov desired to "anoint" his Lord, to set before him a fine table. Post-Communist

Bulgaria was filled with many needs. The poor surrounded him, but his request upon receiving the peace award was for a church organ, to honor the Christ with beautiful music. Some foreigners whispered, "Why was this organ money not given to the poor?" Pastor Beslov, broken in body, walked with the Bulgarian poor, was present to them, and knew their hospitality of the heart. He knew that they too found great joy in participating in the anointing of Jesus.

Judas's words also stole from Mary. Posing as a rescuer of the poor gave him an "honorable" excuse to respond to her in judgment, mocking her gift of anointment, of affirmation, that generous act born from her hospitality of the heart. Not having learned how to give of himself, Judas did not know how to be receptive to others' gifts—gifts offered to himself or to another.

Recently a hospitality committee had the opportunity to plan special events for a meeting of church leaders from across the country. The local people shared joyfully and generously in funding this event. Guests were coming to the table—and the hosts wanted to receive and honor them as "little Christs." But during the meeting one guest, wearing a hand-tailored suit, berated the hosts, "Why was this money not given to the poor?" Perhaps he meant well, but he stole from the hosts. His words of judgment dripped like stains on their hospitality of the heart. One of the dimensions of biblical hospitality is being receptive and creatively responsive to others' gifts—be they sparse or be they nard.

In addition to stealing from the poor and from Mary, Judas's words stole joy—the energy of new life—from the occasion. Mary was trying to bring new life to Jesus in the best way she knew; he had already been threatened and was being hunted. She wanted to do something extra, to bring something special to the table. Jesus understood this and received her kindness. The feelings of sacred festivity in the room float through time, and we can almost feel them ourselves. But Judas changed the mood. He yanked the candles and flowers off the table, so to speak. Dead in soul himself, he did not know how to bring new life to another.

Many of us across our country helped with the food lift during the harsh Russian winter of 1991–92, their first year of transition from the Union of Soviet Socialist Republics to the Commonwealth of Independent States. We bought the listed foods and prepared countless boxes. But from time to time, the list of foods to buy brought a puzzled frown: "Why the big chocolate bar?" Why give something beyond the essentials? Why something extra? (Do we really need to give *parfume* when toilet water will do?) Seared into my memory is the ill, emaciated young Russian woman, beaming with an "Ah-h-h" of new life when she pulled the chocolate bar from her box. WE ARE SCROOGES ~②

Sometimes, as persons and congregations, we assume that there is no place in Christian giving for that something special, that something extra (*lagniappe* is the good Louisiana term). We are willing to help with hunger but do not want to bother with bringing new life. Like Judas, we would yank the candles and the flowers from our hospitality and set a table of "basics only" for those we serve.

The Christian faith is not about either/or. Rarely is our choice truly between feeding the poor and anointing the Lord—with nard or pipe organs or chocolate bars or celebrations at table in his name. Of course we give to the poor and of course we anoint Jesus by offering hospitality of the heart to all those we serve—the poor and the rich. When we practice hospitality in the biblical sense—giving the gift of ourselves, being receptive to the gifts of others, bringing new life to one another as little Christs—it is as though we reach out with Mary, reanointing our Lord. *This Chapter made me feel like the man in the mirror - Guilty.*

RESTORING THE JOY

Scripture: Psalm 51:10-17

As we approach the new millennium, we wring our hands over the way things are. We feel frustrated and paralyzed, bored by routines and overwhelmed by needs. Spiritual hunger springs forth within and around us. We pray with the psalmist: "Restore to me the joy of your salvation, and sustain in me a willing spirit."

Paul says, "The Spirit is life" (Romans 8:10). In Latin, the word is *spiritus*; in Greek, *pneuma*; in Hebrew, *ruah*. These words relate to the wind and the breathing of people. *Spirit* is dynamic, not static. Yet it is unobtrusive, somewhat elusive, evoking a sense of mystery. In his book *We Drink from Our Own Wells*, liberation theologian Gustavo Gutiérrez describes the Spirit as "the power that gives life." The Spirit transforms that familiar sense of void, that sense of something missing, that sense of dreaded deadness, and we taste that integrated wholeness in which we know what it is to be fully *alive*.

In an interview with James M. Wall, the editor of *The Christian Century*, Norman Lear said, "We have got to be willing to talk about God in this country. We've got to be willing to talk of awe, mystery, love." *Awe. Mystery. Love.* These are powerful words, words of spirituality. In our world of instant gratification and electronic communication, we expect to be able to pull through the drive-up window, order spirituality like a hamburger, and drive on out, the soul filled, the deed done. We don't have the time to practice spiritual disciplines nor the patience for the faith journey. According to Matthew Fox, writing in *Creation Spirituality*, "Spirituality is a life-filled path, a spirit-filled way of living." Spirituality is a personal journey, yet a shared pilgrimage.

A few years ago my husband and I happened to be in Chimayo, New Mexico on Good Friday, the day when thousands of Christians make a traditional pilgrimage to *El Santuario de Nuestro Señor de Esquipulas*. From dawn to dark people stream for miles along both sides of the old winding road to the tiny, rough-hewn chapel built in 1816. Some come from Santa Fe; others walk for days from as far away as Albuquerque. The pilgrims are strangers born of different races, starting from different places, going at different paces. Each is on a personal journey; yet all are one through their shared pilgrimage.

Our Lenten journey, both as persons and congregations, is an ongoing Good Friday pilgrimage. We venture forth in the wilderness, open to the Spirit. During the pilgrimage, we find a path worn by the saints who preceded us, a path that connects us with other pilgrims scattered all along the way, a path that gives us direction even in this new day. Fox suggests that "a path is *the way itself*, and every moment on it is a holy moment; a sacred seeing goes on there." Through this sacred seeing we begin to glimpse the essence of awe, mystery, and love. We find ourselves restored and sustained.

═══ ✧ ═══

BETWEEN THE MOMENT OF BREATH and the moment of death is the gift of life as we know it. We are invited to open our eyes and turn that brief span of time into something beautiful for God. We are invited to a dynamic life in the Spirit: to fill our cup and pour out our lives; to experience celebration and suffering, joy and reverence, mystery and awe. We are invited to live faithfully, freely, and fully, witnessing to the wonder of "that last and deepest love that glimmers in our dusk like a pearl, like a face."[6]

Thoughts and Reflections
━━━━━━━━━━━━━━━━━━━━━━━━ ✧

✧ Remember your own baptism. If you were too young to remember it, try to find someone who witnessed the event. Ask, recall, remember. Tell another person about this part of your faith story. Listen to the story of that person's baptism.

✧ What is the importance of your name? What family or faith or historic connections are part of your name?

✧ How do you or could you minister in your workplace? In what ways does the church *send* you into the workplace to minister as a part of the body of Christ? What more might the church do to send you in this path?

✧ Think about one person with whom your relationship tends to grow in a positive direction and one person with whom your relationship tends to grow in a negative direction. How do your responses to the two people differ? What feelings do you have about each? The intent of this pondering is not to bring guilt! You by yourself cannot fix a relationship. Neither is the intent to deal with deep-seated pain. At some points in our life (perhaps throughout our whole life if we do not experience healing), we may know of one person (or more than one) that we are unable to host at our table. Place that one in the hands of the Lord, knowing that the perfect love of Christ will host those whom we, in our imperfection, cannot.

Mike — Support Kairos ministry financially —

BP 50   Quote from
"Wilderness Wandering"
Together we are the
body of Christ.
— Marilyn Brown Oden

8-43

44 — Warner

45-46 —

9/3/47 — M —

9-48 — Ronnie

12-50 — Scott ⟩ Frank H.

9-53 — Beck ⟩

3-56 — Renky ⟩ Chet

3-58 — Ray

3/59 — Sold-Auction — Prudential

4/60 — Merrick Vis. Hosp — Ollie Weber

Eg — Mass Mutual / Danny Charles

N —

6

Wanderering in the Shadow of the Cross

✧

Our wilderness journey now reaches the point where we move from the joyous waving of palm branches to the mournful weeping at the tomb, from "Hosanna!" to "Crucify him!" It is a walk through the dark night of the soul, a journey in the shadow of the cross.

SHOUTING HOSANNA

Scripture: John 12:12-19

The Gospel writer tells us that "the great crowd that had come to the festival heard that Jesus was coming to Jerusalem." A festival crowd is different from a mob. The atmosphere at a festival is one of joy. In *Ministry of the Laity* James D. Anderson and Ezra Earl Jones note the qualities of festivals: A festival includes "friends, neighbors, and strangers. People of all varieties mingle together with a genuine sense of hospitality and without threat or fear." There is "a great profusion of groups and organizations all mixed into the pot—performing, helping, cooking, guiding, selling, parading, sing-ing," and all are "working to a common end and in a spirit of fun and cooperation." A festival has "variety, texture, and color that lend drama and spirit." It is free. "Access is the same for all, no questions asked." Finally, a "sense of common duties and responsibilities prevails." Anderson and Jones suggest that what "is being demonstrated, perhaps in a crowd of many thousands, is the sense of responsibility on the part of each individual for the good of the whole."

Louisiana's many festivals all across the state have enhanced my personal experience with these dynamics. The Washington Parish Fair in Franklinton is a good example. What a joy! At a festival we get out of our lonely little worlds of one and feel that yearned-for sense of belonging.

Congregations can learn from festivals: To provide a warm and open sense of hospitality in which diverse peoples can mingle together in mutual support and care. To facilitate a sense of cooperation, with all members of the body working together for a common end. To be aware of today's complexities and have the courage to respond to the dynamic swirl of the world's variety, texture, and color. To offer the same access for all people, regardless of their status and function beyond the church's walls. To instill a sense of shared responsibility for the good of the whole. Yet these things only touch the surface for communities of faith.

At the festival in Jerusalem that day, the colorful crowd of strangers shared exuberantly in a contagious joy. According to the Gospel of Matthew, Jesus reached Jerusalem by traveling on the Jericho Road from Jericho (770 feet below sea level) through the Mount of Olives region to Jerusalem (2,500 feet above sea level)—a fifteen-mile climb of 3,270 feet. Before entering Jerusalem, Jesus sent two of his disciples for a donkey, which Mark's Gospel says was a colt that had never been ridden. When they returned with it, they put their cloaks over it, and Jesus rode into the city. The crowd spread their cloaks on the road before Jesus. They waved palm branches and shouted "Hosanna!" ("Save us!")

Luke says that "the whole multitude of disciples" shouted, "Blessed is the king who comes in the name of the Lord! Peace in heaven, and glory in the highest heaven!" (Luke 19:38). This displeased some of the Pharisees: "'Teacher, order your disciples to stop.' He answered, 'I tell you, if these were silent, the stones would

Do WE HAVE Pharisees IN OUR MIDST—?
LORD HEAL ME — A PHARISEE —

shout out'" (Luke 19:39-40). When we are silent in our praise and worship, the stones themselves shout God's glory.

But not all is joy on this first Palm Sunday, for it also foretells the passion, suffering, and death of Jesus. This Palm, or Passion, Sunday is a day of ambiguity. In our Lenten journey, we encounter once again our own ambiguity as Christians. We want to participate in an ongoing festival of faith, sharing in the triumphal entry of our Lord into Jerusalem. But we are continually tempted to deny the passion—to deny the suffering and crucifixion that are also part of our faith journey.

This is Holy Week. It takes us through both the joy and the pain. It is a time to pray, to dwell on the scriptures, to reflect on the final events of Jesus' life, and to fast. Yet even as we experience joy and pain, both this Holy Week and in all of life, our joy is more joyful and our pain is less painful because we know how the Story ends. So on this day we take "branches of palm trees and [go] out to meet him, shouting, 'Hosanna! Blessed is the one who comes in the name of the Lord—the King of Israel!'"

HEARING THE WHISPERS

Scripture: Psalm 31:9-16

The psalmist knows the dark night of the soul: "For I hear the whispering of many—terror all around!—as they scheme together against me, as they plot to take my life." As wilderness wanderers we are called to walk through the midnight mist, down the secret pathways to the stark underside of the soul. This journey is also part of our Lenten self-examination.

The dark night of the soul feels like stepping inside the movie *The NeverEnding Story*, where the "Nothing" is shattering everything—"the emptiness that's left. It's like a despair destroying this world." We stand in the abyss, experiencing that three o'clock in the morning kind of loneliness. And as F. Scott Fitzgerald states in *The Crack-Up*, "In a real dark night of the soul, it is always three o'clock in the morning, day after day." Spiritually empty, we find our days filled and our lives unfulfilled. We try to fill the void with more doing or more buying or more drinking or more tranquilizers. But substitutes fail. The movie script warns us: "Listen. The

Nothing will be here any minute." And we ourselves speak the next line: "I will just sit here and let it take me away too."

During this journey through the abyss, life's boundaries move in from the horizon. Limitations cast bars around us. We demote our dreams to fantasies. We drape ourselves in a shroud of guilt over the past and anxiety about the future.

We glance backward at the past, and our "if onlys" engulf us in disappointment and guilt. We face our illusions and become disillusioned. Old grudges resurface—grudges against those who slammed a door to opportunity, those who blocked our way, those whose idle tongues scarred our sacred space. Then the echoing thunder of those grudges is silenced by the flash of lightning on our own irrevocable deeds, those unretrievable words and actions that struck others—spouse, children, parents, church members, colleagues.

We glance ahead at the future, and our "what ifs" envelop us in anxiety. Our future differs from the one we'd earlier envisioned. We tally our goals achieved and dreams denied. On the one hand, unmet dreams force us to face the probability that we will have no opportunity to serve in a "large" way or to do something dramatic and outstanding in our work for the Lord. On the other hand, met—fulfilled—dreams force us to face the reality of descent, for incidents that cause loss of prestige inevitably follow life's peaks. Perhaps the higher the peak, the greater the impact at the thud of descent. Fitzgerald goes on to describe a "blow that comes from within—that you don't feel until it's too late to do anything about it, until you realize with finality that in some regard you will never be as good a [person] again." We feel the inner shock waves as we journey through the midnight mist.

Theologian Thomas C. Oden says in *Two Worlds* that in regard to the future we yearn "to control what is uncontrollable" and in relation to the past "to undo that which is done." We "despair over wishing to form the future and reform the past." But he, like the psalmist who goes on to proclaim his trust in the Lord, does not leave us moaning in despair. He reminds us that through faith we experience the grace of God that transcends our guilt over the past, and through faith we also experience trust in God that transcends our anxiety about the future. Faith heals our brokenness.

achieved
DENIED

Peaks
DESCENT

My first dark night of the soul occurred during a period of being fragmented by the needs of my family, demands of my job, commitments to my church, and the soulful cries for time to write. Somewhere along the way, the light of the Spirit went out of my life. It wasn't sudden—like flipping a switch—but more like a rheostat as the Light gradually dimmed. I'm not sure when it began, really. It's all a blur, a whirl of doing—giving chunks of my life to people and work, breaking myself into pieces like a jigsaw puzzle, not listening to the whispers of the heart, not showing up at "the table." Then the day came when my previous year's "yes" caught up with me. I boarded a plane to lead a retreat, but I had nothing to say. Nothing. I grabbed for the light switch but clutched handfuls of fog. I was empty on the inside—blurred in soul, muddled in mind.

Early the next morning before the first session, I went for a walk alone in the camp setting. The day was misty and gray, a mirror of my soul. I sat down on a boulder beside the stream—the first solitude I'd had in months. I slumped on the rock for a long time. The table felt empty. What if I had drifted too far? What if God had given up on me? What if God didn't love me anymore? Scared and alone, I waited for the "Nothing" to take me away.

And I prayed with the silent, centered fervor that desperation always brings. I don't know how long I sat in the mist before becoming aware of the sun's warmth on my shoulders. But I remember feeling that warmth and looking up and seeing the cosmic breath blowing away the gray clouds. The sun peeked through, above me and within me. In that powerful moment of my dark night, I *experienced* transforming Truth: When we stand in the abyss, absent from God, God is still present with us—unseen. God's love follows us—unclaimed. God's word is with us—unheard. We can ignore God's love, but we can never escape it.

As we stumble through the cobwebs in the midnight mist, filled with loneliness and despair and bent double by our burdens, the whisper of God's love can penetrate the mist—even from the underside of the soul. We know the outcome of the Story. We do not have to remain entombed in the dark night. We do not have to wrap ourselves in the graveclothes of self-pity, blame, bitterness, cynicism, suspicion, vengeance. We do not have to become like the sea creatures of the deep who make bizarre adaptations to survive severe cold, pressure, and lightlessness. We are the Easter people, called "out of darkness into his marvelous light" (1 Peter 2:9).

The dark night of the soul is temporary. It comes as a challenge to grow, bringing new sight that becomes insight. In his light, we walk forward in resurrection—a new creation. We listen for the sounds of God's presence, and it sings to us like a soft lullaby or vibrates in us like a *tutti* all-stops-pulled organ crescendo. We look for the signs of God's presence and find that presence everywhere. We see it in the liturgical colors of the earth—the royal purple of the crepe myrtle, the evergreen branches of the pine tree, the scarlet shimmering of the wild flowers. We see God's presence in the loftiness of the white half-moon lingering in the new dawn sky and in the earthiness of the rushing ants on their dusty mound. God is present in all that we can see and smell, touch and hear—and in all that is beyond our senses. God is present in all that we know—and in all that is beyond our knowing. When we hear the third chime of the clock in the 3 A.M. mist, we remember that on the third day the stone was rolled away!

Q. Discuss ?
26:13

SLEEPING WHILE JESUS GRIEVES

Scripture: Matthew 26–27
(Passion Narrative of Matthew)

David Bosch in *Transforming Mission* suggests that Matthew's Gospel was written "to provide guidance to a community in crisis on how it should understand its calling and mission." We surely need that guidance today! The Gospel tells us that Jesus said to the disciples in Gethsemane, "'I am deeply grieved, even to death; remain here, and stay awake with me.' . . . Then he came to the disciples and found them sleeping." As the church we have been sleeping while Jesus grieves. We pushed back from the table and took a nap.

Sleeping while Jesus grieves, we have fractured oneness in Spirit. To be one in the Spirit does not mean that we are all alike, that we all agree or are compatible. We come together into community on the Sabbath from big houses, small ones, condos, parsonages, apartments, public housing, dorm rooms, and shelters. Behind those doors, we leave varying degrees of loneliness, stability,

> OR BLINK AT THE LIGHT

support, security, and care. As we pass through the open doors into the church, some of us smile, others frown, and a few blink back the tears. Some want to serve, others to be served, and a few simply hope to survive. Each one of us is unique and precious in God's eyes. Each has individual values, experiences, ideas, advantages, and flaws; each has different levels of sensitivity and awareness, philosophies and purposes, talents and abilities.

Some of us, both clergy and lay, have deep and abiding faith because we believe in biblical miracles as literal events and we believe that God keeps a running score of our kind and evil deeds and rewards the righteous with good things—and we know we are *right*! We know that no one else with any other view can truly live the faith—for God sits *only* at our table. Likewise some of us, both clergy and lay, have deep and abiding faith without believing in biblical miracles as literal events or that God keeps a running score of our kind and evil deeds, and rewards the righteous with good things—and we know we are *right*! We know that no one else with any other view can truly live the faith—for God sits *only* at our table.

Paul said, "There is no longer Jew or Greek, there is no longer slave or free, there is no longer male and female; for all of you are one in Christ Jesus" (Galatians 3:28). There is no longer liberal or fundamentalist, evangelical or social activist, creationist or evolutionist, left or right, for we are all one in Christ. In "Invitation to the Spiritual Life" Nouwen assures us that the "mystery of community is precisely that it embraces *all* people, whatever their individual differences may be." Our oneness is not in sameness but in Spirit.

Sleeping while Jesus grieves, we—both clergy and laity—have divided the *laos*, the people of God. Some clergy point their fingers at the laity: *Laypersons aren't what they used to be! They seem more interested in comfort than commitment, more concerned with talking than doing, and they take the church for granted instead of giving it first place. They care more about what the church can do for them than what they can do for others. What happened to the God-fearing, dedicated laity of the past?*

And some laypersons point back at the clergy: *Pastors aren't what they used to be! They seem more interested in salary than spirituality, more concerned with expediency than evangelism, and they run the church like a business instead of by the Bible. What happened to the God-fearing, dedicated clergy of the past?* Divided and divisive, we do the dance of death. We miss the opportunity to *be* the church. To paraphrase Paul once more, there is no longer clergy or lay; we are all one in our baptism.

Sleeping while Jesus grieves, we have ignored his new commandment: "Love one another." Morton Kelsey in *The Other Side of Silence* offers a helpful view of the difference between Christian and Eastern meditation: Whereas Eastern meditation views reality as a "pool of cosmic consciousness in which one seeks to lose identity," Christian meditation sees ultimate reality as "a Lover to whom one responds." As Christians, we respond to the loving God.

According to Nouwen, to be obedient means to be constantly attentive to the "active presence of God and to allow [God], who is only love, to be the source as well as the goal of all we think, say and do." The basic Lenten questions of self-examination center on the journey inward: *Do you love the Lord your God with all your heart, soul, and mind?* And on the journey outward: *Do you love your neighbor as yourself?*

God loves us all. We all commune at the Lord's table, and we all reflect our faith by our loving behavior toward others. Robert N. Bellah says that if the church is to be the church, it must "hold up an alternative vision of reality, to give witness to what, as best we can discern it, God is saying to the world today" (from "Leadership Viewed from the Vantage Point of American Culture"). As we stay awake with Jesus in today's Gethsemane times, watching and listening, we can begin to grasp that alternative vision.

this paragraph was different to!! I did not comprehen

WAKENING OUR EARS AND BENDING OUR KNEES

Scripture: Isaiah 50:4-9; Philippians 2:5-11

God has placed us in a world forged from escalating change. It isn't the world we expected nor prepared for as the church. Old visions are obsolete, and new visions are in the fetal stage—in process but unborn. Yet we need not tremble in confusion, for the Holy One is there before us, calling us toward this "new thing."

Isaiah whispers to us: "Morning by morning he wakens—wakens my ear to listen as those who are taught." We have been taught the

Story. But for many it lives only in memory. In an article in *The New Yorker*, a former Methodist reflects on his spiritual grounding as a child when reverence and prayer were an integral part of his life. He yearns for that dimension once more, but he's no longer comfortable with it. He feels his guests around the table wouldn't understand. He keeps his spiritual longing in the silence of his heart.

In *Telling Secrets* Buechner's words rise from the page and haunt our own silence: "Their faith itself, if they happen to have any, is one of the secrets that they have kept so long that it might almost as well not exist." That early spiritual grounding, which once was taken for granted has been locked in silent memory all across our country. This silence has left generations of children to grow up without even the memory but not without a sense that something is missing in their lives—thus the rising "spirituality" market in the secular world. (NEED FOR WITNESSING)

Seminaries, well-intentioned but with unawakened ears, led in the shift away from spirituality. Paul Wilkes notes in "The Hands That Would Shape Our Souls" in *The Atlantic* that in the fifties, generally seminaries began dividing theological education into specialized disciplines. Since "spiritual life could not be quantified, charted, assessed," it was "pronounced personal and left up to the individual." With increasing emphasis on the academic elements, personal spirituality was not considered "especially relevant."

We get a further glimpse through the eyes of Buechner who comments on the students in his preaching class in the early eighties: "To attend a divinity school when you did not believe in divinity involved a peculiarly depressing form of bankruptcy, and there were times as I wandered through those corridors that I felt a little like Alice on the far side of the looking glass." Academic theology has been admirably addressed but oftentimes severed from the faith journey—like earthbound instructors teaching astronauts the various aspects of the space journey: their words are important, their knowledge essential, but the experience itself is missing. With the recent hunger for spirituality, many (most?) seminaries have opened their ears and dusted off the word *spiritual*—now using it without a stammer or a blush.

In *The Dream of the Earth* Thomas Berry states that "the deepest crises experienced by any society are those moments of change when the story becomes inadequate for meeting the survival demands of a present situation." He sees us in that kind of crisis now, suggesting that we no longer know the meaning of our Story or how to benefit from its guidance. Our timeless Story *is* adequate for our day. What is *in*adequate is the way we sometimes tell it.

Paul says that God gave Christ Jesus "the name that is above every name, so that at the name of Jesus every knee should bend, . . . and every tongue should confess that Jesus Christ is Lord." So often we tell our Story without bending our knees, losing the reverence, the mystery.

In *Space and Light* Marius von Senden describes patients, blind from birth, who upon receiving sight do not at first realize that "a larger object (a chair) can mask a smaller one (a dog), or that the latter can still be present even though it is not directly seen." We are like those newly sighted patients. Modern science, which has radically changed from the old science at the time of Christ (and which will also be radically changed by future science) looms so large before us that we fail to perceive the presence of Mystery beyond it.

The prophets and apostles told the Story out of the trappings of their culture, but they transcended that culture by keeping before them the vision of the new and holy future that could be shaped by following the loving Christ. For Christians who are weaving our way through the minefields of our day, the task is not defense of the Holy One but transcendence of the unholy.

It is Jesus Christ who is the same yesterday, today, and tomorrow—not the world or the church, whose task is to be the loving face and healing hands of Christ in God's changing world. At this moment in time the world desperately needs the renewal of individual faith, the strengthening of communities of faith, the relating of Christ's teachings to the global community, and the honoring of God's good earth. As we tiptoe through the wilderness in the shadow of the cross, we hear Isaiah's whisperings and Paul's proclamation. We waken our ears and bend our knees, telling the old Story in a new way.

PREPARING THE TABLE

Scripture: Mark 14–15
(Passion Narrative of Mark)

The disciples walk along with Jesus as they have many times before. They don't know of the suffering he will endure this week. They don't know they are walking in the shadow of the cross. They don't know that the end of the story is upon them and that in the ending is the beginning of the new covenant.

They are traveling from Bethany (probably the present-day village of Al-ʻAzariyeh) to Jerusalem. It is a journey of about two miles across the Mount of Olives, a ridge of hills overlooking the old city. The ridge has three summits. The second summit, directly across the Kidron Valley east of Jerusalem, is the Mount of Olives proper, with an altitude of 2,660 feet. The village of Bethany is on the farther downslope of the southeast subsidiary ridge.[1] Jesus and the disciples walk along the steep bank. Their feet kick up dust as they step, and the way is rocky. Perhaps the disciples question the Teacher. Perhaps they talk and laugh. Perhaps they feel the heavy-heartedness of Jesus.

Except one. Judas Iscariot is busy making plans with the chief priests—offering to betray Jesus—and is offered a reward in return.

Jesus sends two disciples ahead to prepare for the Passover, a family celebration commemorating the freedom and redemption of the Jewish people. Jesus instructs the two to "say to the owner of the house, 'The Teacher asks, Where is my guest room where I may eat the Passover with my disciples?' . . . Make preparations for us there" (Mark 14:14, 15).

The sun goes down, and Jesus and the twelve gather at the table in the large room. The clay oil lamps are lit, casting flickering shadows on the table and blending with the aroma of lamb, unleavened bread, and wine. Perhaps some of the disciples hesitate as they take their places at the table, each longing to be the ones who sit near Jesus. As they eat, Jesus makes a somber announcement that one of them will betray him. Going around the table one after another, they respond, "Surely, not I?" (The question mark shows that they *ask* if they are the betrayer rather than *declare* their loyalty.)

Then according to John's Gospel (and only John's, which differs in many ways from Mark), Jesus rises from the table and begins to wash and wipe the disciples' feet, an act of humility and servanthood. Peter resists, then offers his hands and head also. Afterward Jesus admonishes his disciples to do as he has done. He also gives them a new commandment: "Love one another."

According to the accounts of Matthew, Mark, and Luke, Jesus breaks the bread and blesses it and offers it to them, a symbol of his body. In the common is the holy. Then Jesus takes the cup, gives thanks, and all of them drink from it, a symbol of his blood of the new covenant, poured out for many. And in that precious moment, Jesus gives the church the sacrament of the Lord's Supper.

On this Holy Thursday, we too are in a steep part of our Lenten wilderness journey. We have formed groups along the way, joining together for this part of our pilgrimage. The dust rises as we walk, and some of us are weary. Unlike Jesus' disciples, we know what is ahead, and we walk somberly. Soon our journey through the wilderness will end, but not yet. Crucifixion precedes resurrection. We are not thinking now, not trying to learn anything, not confessing, not envisioning, not examining ourselves, not seeking renewal. We are undistracted and centered, walking with our Lord in the shadow of the cross.

This time we do not veer off from the faith journey. *This* time we do not accompany Judas. *This* time we cannot be bought, and we do not involve ourselves in acts of betrayal.

Jesus sends us ahead to prepare the table. We know how to do it. We've found a space and prepared the table many times before—not only when we've come to the table in our special place of solitude, but also when family and friends have gathered around the table for holiday (holy-day) feasts. Yet tonight is different. Already we can feel it. We make these preparations in our hearts.

Darkness falls and we gather at the church, finding our places on this Holy Thursday. Jesus' announcement of betrayal runs through our mind. Our well-intentioned soul responds, "Surely, not I?"—and the question mark belies our confidence. How much we love him! But how hard it is to serve him faithfully!

Perhaps we rise for a foot-washing service. Perhaps not. But some of us have done this in the past. A person washes our feet, and then we wash another's. Like Peter, we cannot imagine the Lord's washing our feet! It is difficult to allow another to tend our feet, much easier on the ego to be the active one doing the washing—giving the gift—than the passive one being washed. Whether or not we wash one another's feet, we understand the meaning: To follow Jesus is to get up from the table to perform sacrificial service—and also to be willing to receive sacrificial gifts from others. In this way—and in many other ways—we show love to one another.

And then it is time for the Lord's Supper. We look toward the altar with the Lord's table beautifully prepared with the best that we have. The table is covered with a white damask cloth, a memorial gift used only for Holy Communion. Beside the gold-plated cross, the symbolic light of the world flickers in two false candles, constant in size with no messy drips. Our eyes shift to the silk flowers whose blooms, scentless and seedless, won't wilt or die. The pastor breaks the bread and blesses it, saying the words of old. Then as the pastor reaches across the chalice to set down the bread, the long full sleeves of the robe drag, and one sleeve catches on the chalice and tips it. There is just an instant before the chalice is uprighted.

But in that instant, the red wine spills. It runs across the beautiful cloth and seeps under the candlesticks and reaches the cross. It begins to bleed down the front overhang of the white cloth. Everyone in the congregation can see the spilled blood of Christ dripping, staining, trickling where it will. In the midst of the high holy feast is a lowly holy error. The blood of Christ is *poured* out. And perhaps there is a smile as the Holy One welcomes us to the table, for the tipped chalice co-incidentally reminds us that the blood of Christ—that amazing love of the new covenant—cannot be controlled, restrained, confined, contained.

WATCHING FROM A DISTANCE

Scripture: Luke 22–23
(Passion Narrative of Luke)

According to Luke, jealousy and competition arise among the disciples even around the table following the Passover meal together. Jesus, who has so little time left, not only has to deal with betrayal and the agony ahead but also with the dispute among his little band about who is the greatest. Peter proclaims confidently that he is ready to go with the Lord "to prison and to death!" (exclamation point), and Jesus tells Peter that he will deny him three times. Then Jesus goes to the Mount of Olives, and the disciples follow him. He withdraws "about a stone's throw away," kneels, and prays—while the disciples sleep.

Judas leads a crowd to Jesus, offering the kiss of betrayal. One of Jesus' followers, wanting to protect Jesus, cuts off the right ear of the high priest's slave. Jesus says, "No more of this!" and heals the wounded one. Then they seize Jesus and take him to the high priest's house. Peter follows at a distance and then sits among the crowd who have kindled a fire against the cold night. Even in the dancing shadows of the flames, some of them recognize Peter as one who has been with Jesus. And Peter replies—three different times—that he does not know the man. The cock crows, Jesus turns and looks at him, and Peter departs, weeping bitterly.

As soon as day comes—this cruel Friday morning that continues to shake the world—Jesus is brought before the council of the elders, then taken to Pilate with the accusation that "He stirs up the people by teaching." When Pilate learns that Jesus is a Galilean, he sends him to Herod, who is in Jerusalem at this time. Herod is glad to see Jesus; he's heard of him and wants to see some magic. Jesus offers no response to Herod, so Herod and his soldiers mock Jesus. Herod robes him elegantly and sends him back to Pilate. Again Pilate finds no guilt in Jesus and three times tells "the chief priest, the leaders, and the people" that he will have Jesus flogged and release him. But they demand "with loud shouts that he should be crucified; and their voices prevailed"; Pilate hands Jesus over to them.

Simon of Cyrene carries the cross for Jesus to the place of The Skull, out from the city. And there Jesus is crucified between two criminals, one who derides him and one who asks for remembrance and is promised Jesus' presence. At noon darkness falls until three o'clock. Jesus breathes his last. The crowds who have gathered to see "this spectacle" return home, mourning. But all Jesus' "acquaintances, including the women who had followed him from Galilee, stood at a distance, watching these things."

We too watch these events from a distance and witness their recurrence in our day. Like the disciples, we act out of jealousy and competition both when we walk in the world and when we sit at the table. Like Peter, we proclaim with our words that we will follow Jesus—even to prison and to death. But in the shadows of the flames, we deny knowing him. Our denial takes the form of unkind words, exploitative deeds, and evil thoughts. Or it takes the form of harried fragmentation that leaves us no time and space for spiritual renewal. Or it takes the form of silent omission.

Like the well-meaning man who cut off the ear, we do some dreadful things under the guise of defending our Lord. (How audacious that we even consider that the Lord needs our protection!) Throughout the world we slaughter others who differ in faith. In our country we form "Christian" militias and to-the-death cults. We justify murder for moral causes like right-to-life. We form into camps and attempt to outshout and outmaneuver one another in defense of Christianity. And Jesus Christ, our Lord and Savior, says, "No more of this!" He restores the ear of the broken one, and that lesson should open the ears of all Christians to his commandment: "Love one another." *fear / love*

Like the people on that Friday morning long ago, we fear one another rather than love one another. We huddle into groups and hurl accusations at others for stirring up things by teaching a new way. Like Herod, we seek magic and signs and take comfort in superstitious and undisciplined faith. Also like Herod, we clothe the body of Christ in elegance, not understanding that without our hearts our beautiful structures mock the Christ. As with Pilate, shouting mobs still prevail over reason. And on this Friday morning, this Good Friday morning, we crucify our Lord.

MOURNING THE DARKNESS

Scripture: John 13; 18–19
(Passion Narrative of John)

The Gospel of John says:
"Since it was the Jewish
day of Preparation,
and the tomb was nearby
they laid Jesus there." Woe! —
Our Lord lies in the tomb.

On this Jewish Sabbath,
this holy day of rest,
the women must wait to
bring spices and ointments
to care for his body. ⸺
Our Lord lies in the tomb.

Mournful Saturday morn.
Thunder rolls a loud dirge
in the darkest of skies.
The earth is no-color,
the gray essence of grief. ⸺
Our Lord lies in the tomb.

The palm branches wither.
The gnarled olive tree weeps
that Jesus knelt beneath
in the Garden of Geth-
semane, praying, grieved. ⸺
Our Lord lies in the tomb.

We see thirty pieces
of silver. The cross. Sharp
swords. The crown of thorns. The
place of The Skull, tears dripping down its hollow eyes. ⸺
Our Lord lies in the tomb.

This is the day of earth's
mourning. The darkest day
of Sheol. The day the
Gospels omit. This is
the day of God's silence. ⸺
Our Lord lies in the tomb.

Thoughts and Reflections

- ✧ How does worship in your church resemble a festival? If hospitality and joy are not obvious to all, what will you do to help prepare the festival of worship?
- ✧ How do you respond to the idea of sleeping in the garden while Jesus grieves? What enables us to be present and attentive in today's Gethsemane? How can the disciplines of Lent enable us to proclaim Jesus' vision of God's world?
- ✧ How can you respond to the spiritual hunger of the world? In what directions do you see the mission and ministry of the church shifting to respond to that spiritual hunger?
- ✧ Think about Herod's desire to see signs and magic. What good news can we offer to those today who want to see signs and magic?
- ✧ Take five minutes to draw or write a response to "Mourning the Darkness." Tell a friend about this poem and your response to it. Talk with your study group about the spiritual significance of the Saturday of Holy Week.

7

Wanderers Awakened!

Scripture: Matthew 28:1-7; Mark 16:1-4;
Luke 24:1-5; John 20:11-18

Christ is risen!
Christ is risen indeed!

For two millennia Christians throughout the world have greeted one another on Easter morning with these words. As we say them again on this glorious day of Resurrection, they not only echo from the past but also ripple into the third millennium and on into the fourth.

Christ is risen!
Christ is risen indeed!

Christ is risen in the world. The sun rises and wakens the earth. The birds play flute. The flowers open in antiphonal anthems. The lichens on the ancient rocks chant in praise. The Light has come into the darkness! The divine mystery enfolds us, lifts us!

Christ is risen!
Christ is risen indeed!

Christ is risen in our lives. Nothing will ever be quite the same again. The Holy Spirit works within us, through us, and around us. The Christ has shared the secrets of the faith-filled life, and we journey in a new kind of light, in a new kind of living, in a new kind of giving that brings life to others and to ourselves. Deeply and joyfully we renew our baptismal vows, returning to the Holy One with all our hearts.

Christ is risen!
Christ is risen indeed!

Christ is risen in the church. Our Sabbath moves from the last day of the week to the first, the day of Resurrection. We draw to-gether—together in community in the name of Jesus Christ, together as his body. We have been given light, a light than can never be extinguished. We have been given the Word, a Word of hope and love that teaches us how to live together. We have been given water, the water of baptism that makes us new creatures in Christ. We have been given the Eucharist, the Lord's Supper, which welcomes all believers to God's table. We worship and praise and serve. We seek and teach and reach. We hold hands as communities of faith around God's earth, not making a chain that shuts others out but encircling all God's people with the empowering light of holy love. We go to the edge and dare to leap; and miracles of miracles, we find that feeble as we are, together we can soar!

Christ is risen!
Christ is risen indeed!
Alleluia!

God loves us so much that the Son was given that we might have life. We are called by our baptism to be instruments of that same love. On this glorious Easter morning we come out from the wilderness back into the world, saying with the poet George Herbert: "Awake, my lute, and struggle for thy part."

Guides for Wanderers

GUIDE FOR INDIVIDUAL LENTEN PILGRIMAGE

The Introduction suggests a format for reading the book. You may choose to follow your soul in your own reflections on the scriptures and the book or use the following outline as a "guided" pilgrimage:

✧ **Recentering through silence and prayer**
You may wish to try praying in the various ways noted in PRAYER, chapter 4.

✧ **Reading and reflecting on the scriptures**
Consider reading some of the scriptures in the various ways noted in SCRIPTURE, chapter 2.

✧ **Reading *Wilderness Wanderings***
Read one chapter a week during Lent. Read chapter 7 on Easter.

✧ **Reflecting on the questions in THOUGHTS AND REFLECTIONS at the end of each chapter**

✧ **Repenting**
Kathleen Norris in her book *Dakota* quotes a contemporary monk who suggests that repentance has to do with renouncing our narrow human views that are too small for God's mystery. Think about a time when something happened in the congregation or the denomination that triggered a negative feeling in you. If your feeling was intense, reflect on whether the source of your feeling could have been a view too narrow for God's mystery.

✧ **Receiving and celebrating God's grace**
Remember that God accepts, forgives, and loves you.

✧ **Renewing discipleship**
You may wish to follow relevant parts of RENEWING DISCIPLESHIP, found in this guide.

✧ **Returning to God's world with a prayerful heart**

Guide for Group Lenten Pilgrimage

Our Lenten pilgrimage is a wandering, a process in which we trust the Holy Spirit with our personal and communal destination. As *Wanderers* in community, we covenant together. Our covenant is not to the group or to the book. It is a covenant to our pilgrimage of faith in Jesus Christ, and this covenant is *with* one another. In this covenant we support one another in our pilgrimage, and we hold one another accountable to it. We express this covenant:

✧ By coming to "the table" individually each day, praying and reading the scriptures;

✧ By coming to "the table" weekly with our *Wilderness Wanderings* sojourners, viewing this as sacred time in communion with God and one another;

✧ By reading the designated chapter of *Wilderness Wanderings* (I recommend reading portions daily beginning with chapter 2);

✧ By attending each session and being present with our minds and our hearts—not having an out-of-body experience!

✧ By being open to the breath of the Spirit and expecting to grow as persons and as a group.

As *Wanderers* we will honor these community courtesies:

✧ To listen in love, without disapproval of other *Wanderers* and to share in truth (as we perceive it);

✧ To value individual uniqueness and welcome fresh perspectives, recognizing that richness of diversity helps us grow;

✧ To face differences openly, treating each other with respect and applying the RSV translation of Isaiah 1:18: "Come now, let us reason together" rather than that of the NRSV: "Come now, let us argue it out"!

✧ To honor requests for confidentiality.

A WORD FOR LEADERS

The primary task of the leader is not to teach but to be in pilgrimage with the other *Wanderers* and to facilitate the journey. The leader has six major responsibilities:

1. To begin and end each session on time.
2. To be sure everyone understands the format for reading the book and which chapter is to be read each week.
3. To follow the guide when appropriate for the group but not to see it as an "assignment" to be accomplished. Trust where the Spirit leads the *Wanderers*.
4. To facilitate group sharing so no one dominates, and everyone has equal opportunities to share without feeling pressured to do so. (A group of ten people would mean that each person's fair share—including the leader—is ten percent of the allotted time.)
5. To set the tone for the sessions as a warm, comfortable, and stimulating place to be. A centering symbol might help (for example, lighting a candle upon completion of the "Reconnecting" before moving into the "Recentering" time).
6. To close each session on a hopeful, accepting, caring note.

Since each person is a unique creation of God, we celebrate our differences rather than fear them. Though the silence together may feel a bit uneasy in the beginning, we will become more comfortable with it as the pilgrimage continues.

INTRODUCTORY SESSION
(For a seven-session pilgrimage beginning Ash Wednesday)

PREPARING FOR THE PILGRIMAGE

✧ Distribute the books.

✧ Go around the circle, stating the name you prefer that persons call you and saying aloud what the book cover brings to mind.

✧ Go around again (stating your name once more) and tell something you look forward to in participating in *Wanderers* during this Lenten season.

✧ Discuss the format for the sessions and for reading the book. (See the Introduction.)

✧ Call attention to the aspects of the covenant (page 122).

ENTERING THE WILDERNESS

✧ **Recentering through prayer** for guidance and a time of silence.

✧ **Reading the scripture**: Joel 2:1-2, 12-17.

✧ **Thinking and reflecting**, allowing the questions at the end of the chapter to guide your discussion.

✧ **Receiving and celebrating God's grace**
Go around the circle receiving and giving a word of grace.

✧ **Renewing discipleship:** Begin the wilderness journey of praying, reading the scriptures, and reading the book (chapter 1 for next week).

✧ **Returning to God's world**
Close with prayer, sending the *Wanderers* forth with prayerful hearts into God's world.

---

1. WANDERING IN THE WILDERNESS
(First week in Lent)

For a six-session pilgrimage group: Distribute books prior to this session and assign chapter 1 as reading for the first session. See "Preparing for the Pilgrimage" in the introductory session.

✧ **Reconnecting with one another** (if this is the second session)

✧ **Recentering through prayer** for guidance and a time of silence.

✧ **Reading the scripture**: Matthew 6:1-6, 19-21
  (The discussion guide is an adaptation of a model for Bible study from the Lumko Missiological Institute of South Africa via the base communities of South Africa.)
  One person reads the passage aloud.
  What word stood out to you? Go around the circle and share *one word* (not one verse but *one word*!) that stood out to you. (Persons may mention the same word.)
  Reread the passage (by a person of a different gender, race, or generation if possible).
  Where does this passage touch your life today? Go around the circle again and share in *one phrase* (not one sentence but *one phrase*) where this passage touches your life today.
  Reread the passage (by a third reader).
  What or how is God inviting you to change in the immediate future? Go around the circle again and, based upon what persons have heard and said, share in *one sentence* (not one paragraph but *one sentence*) what or how is God inviting you to change in the immediate future.
  Go around the circle and pray (by name) for the *Wanderer* seated to your right—pray for his or her desired change (naming that change). During this week, each person prays that same prayer daily for that *Wanderer*.

✧ **Thinking and reflecting**
  Allow the questions at the end of the chapter to guide your discussion.

✧ **Repenting**

Kathleen Norris in her book *Dakota* quotes a contemporary monk who suggests that repentance has to do with renouncing our narrow human views that are too small for God's mystery. Think about a time when something happened in the congregation or the denomination that triggered a negative feeling in you. If your feeling was intense, reflect on whether the source of your feeling could have been a view that is perhaps too narrow for God's mystery. Reflect in silence for a few moments. *Do not discuss.*

✧ **Receiving and celebrating God's grace**

Go around the circle, receiving and giving a word of grace. Words or gestures of acceptance, forgiveness, assurance, and thanksgiving are appropriate ways to receive and celebrate grace.

✧ **Renewing discipleship**

- Continue the wilderness journey of praying, reading the scripture, and reading *Wilderness Wanderings* (chapter 2 for next week).
- Pray daily for the *Wanderer* (by name) you prayed for when the scripture was read.
- Try journaling as part of your pilgrimage by recording thoughts, images, and signposts of your wilderness wanderings. (This journaling might take the form of a page a day, a poem, a song, a sketch, or a painting.)

✧ **Returning to God's world**

Close with prayer, sending the *Wanderers* forth with prayerful hearts into God's world.

---

2. WANDERERS CALLED BY CHRIST
(Second week in Lent)

✧ **Reconnecting with one another**

✧ **Recentering through prayer** for guidance and a time of silence

✧ **Reading the scripture**: Luke 4:1-2, 5-9

Think about the small percentage of Judeo-Christian history during which the people of faith have been able to read their own Book. Listen to the reading of the scripture as though you are a Christian before the time of Gutenberg and his printing press: You have no Bible; you will never have one. Your only access to the scriptures is by *hearing* them read aloud. Come to the scripture reading with that perspective. After the reading, consider what that was like for you.

✧ **Thinking and reflecting**

Allow the questions at the end of the chapter to guide your discussion.

✧ **Repenting**

Answer in your heart, reflecting silently after each question: Did you keep your covenant with this group this week to show up at "the table" daily to pray and read the scripture? Did you read chapter 2 of the book? Did you ponder whether some of your religious views are too narrow for God's mystery? Did you pray daily for the *Wanderer* you named last week? Did you follow a step or two in the direction the scripture led you? Would anyone like to share something meaningful about your pilgrimage?

✧ **Receiving and celebrating God's grace**

Go to the person who prayed for you and to the person for whom you prayed, receiving and giving a word of grace.

✧ **Renewing discipleship**

- Go around the circle and share which of the spiritual disciplines you would like most to grow in.
- Go around the circle again and pray (by name) for the *Wanderer* sitting to your left—praying for his or her progress in that spiritual discipline (naming it aloud). During

this week, pray that same prayer daily for that *Wanderer*.

- Continue the wilderness journey of praying, reading the scripture, and reading *Wilderness Wanderings* (chapter 3 for next week).
- Try to make a place for solitude. Figure out how to make one this week—just a tiny little space.
- Continue meaningful journaling.
- Try reading the scriptures at least once this week in one of the ways described in SCRIPTURE in chapter 2.

✧ **Returning to God's world**

Close with a prayer, sending the *Wanderers* forth with prayerful hearts into God's world.

3. WANDERERS WITH HALOS AND CLAY FEET
(Third Week in Lent)

✧ **Reconnecting with one another**
✧ **Recentering through prayer** for guidance and a time of silence
✧ **Reading the scripture**: Colossians 3:12-17
As the scripture is read, let's consider the reflective meditation of Saint Ignatius and place ourselves mentally in God's presence, asking ourselves these questions:
- Who is speaking to me?
- What does this mean to me?
- Where does this apply to my life?
- How and when do I respond?

Discuss the scripture based on the questions of Saint Ignatius. Go around the circle and tell in which (if any) of these areas you would like to be better "clothed."
✧ **Thinking and reflecting**
Allow the questions at the end of the chapter to guide your discussion.
✧ **Repenting**
Answer in your heart, reflecting silently after each question: Did you keep your covenant with this group this week to show up at "the table" daily to pray and read the scripture? Did you read chapter 3 of the book? Did you ponder whether some of your religious views are too narrow for God's mystery? Did you pray daily for the *Wanderer* you named last week? Did you make a place for solitude? Did you take a step toward the spiritual discipline you desired? Would anyone like to share something meaningful about your pilgrimage?
✧ **Receiving and celebrating God's grace**
Go to the person who prayed for you and to the person for whom you prayed, receiving and giving a word of grace.

✧ **Renewing discipleship**

- Continue the wilderness journey of praying, reading the scripture, and reading *Wilderness Wanderings* (chapter 4 for next week).
- Pray for each *Wanderer* by name, that each of us may take bold steps this week on our Lenten pilgrimage of faith in Jesus Christ.
- Continue to journal if it is meaningful to your pilgrimage.
- Move forward in the direction you felt led two weeks ago.
- Continue to take steps in the spiritual disciplines.
- Listen to your soul and trust the voice that comes from deep within—that voice you hear at "the table."
- "Clothe" yourself each morning as you dress in the quality you chose from the Colossians scripture.
- Repeat Psalm 27:13 silently several times each day this week: "I believe that I shall see the goodness of the Lord in the land of the living." Gifts of relationships and nature abound in our lives, but we generally miss them. Keep this scripture in mind and look for "the gift of the day."

✧ **Returning to God's world**

Close with prayer, sending the *Wanderers* forth with prayerful hearts into God's world.

4. WORDS FOR WANDERERS
(Fourth week in Lent)

✧ **Reconnecting with one another**

✧ **Recentering through prayer** for guidance and a time of silence

✧ **Reading the scripture**: John 9:1-11

One way to read scripture is to place ourselves in them—becoming participants instead of observers. As the scripture is read, let's open our imagination and senses (seeing, hearing, smelling, touching, tasting) and *be* there. Then raise these questions after the scripture is read: What did you see? hear? smell? What textures or temperatures did you sense? What could you taste?

✧ **Thinking and reflecting**

Allow the questions at the end of the chapter to guide your discussion.

✧ **Repenting**

Answer in your heart, reflecting silently after each question: Did you keep your covenant with this group this week to show up at "the table" daily to pray and read the scripture? Did you ponder whether some of your religious views are too narrow for God's mystery? Are you taking steps forward in the spiritual disciplines? Did you listen to that deep place in your soul and make any kind of response? Did you pray daily for each *Wanderer* by name? Did you remember each morning to "clothe" yourself in the quality you chose from Colossians? Did you remember to repeat Psalm 27:13 frequently and look for the "gift of the day"? After silent reflection, ask, "Would anyone like to share any 'gift of the day' you received this week? Would anyone like to share something meaningful about your pilgrimage?"

✧ **Receiving and celebrating God's grace**

Go around the circle, receiving and giving a word of grace.

✧ Renewing discipleship

- Continue the wilderness journey of praying, reading the scripture, and reading *Wilderness Wanderings* (chapter 5 for next week).
- Continue to journal if it is meaningful to your pilgrimage.
- Continue to take steps in the spiritual disciplines.
- Continue to pray for each *Wanderer* by name.
- Try praying in one of the ways new to you described in PRAYER in chapter 4.
- Be "playful" with God at least once this week.
- Listen for opportunities to bless another's life. That opportunity may not be given but *listen* for it.
- Be present to someone this week who needs your presence.
- Become attuned to your own perceptions this week and be open to other options.
- Think about our Lord's suffering every time you see a cross this week, whether in a church, on a sign, around someone's neck. Realize that his suffering was for you and ponder what that means for your life.

✧ Returning to God's world

Close with prayer, sending the *Wanderers* forth with prayerful hearts into God's world.

(***Note to the leader:*** Wanderers *will need to have access to the same version of the Bible for the scripture reading the next session.*)

5. WITNESSING TO THE WONDER
(Fifth week in Lent)

✧ **Reconnecting with one another**
✧ **Recentering through prayer** for guidance and a time of silence
✧ **Reading the scripture**: Psalm 51:6-12
Nouwen suggests that we look at a scripture and listen to it with our inner eyes and ears. Let's both look at and listen to this scripture as we read it aloud together. When you see this scripture with your inner eye and listen to it with your inner ear, how does it relate to your own wilderness wandering during this Lenten season?
✧ **Thinking and reflecting**
Allow the questions at the end of the chapter to guide your discussion.
✧ **Repenting**
Answer in your heart, reflecting silently after each question: Did you keep your covenant with this group this week to show up at "the table" daily to pray and read the scripture? Did you read chapter 5 of the book? Did you have an opportunity to bless another's life? Were you present to someone this week who needed your presence? Did the crosses you saw this week remind you to consider what our Lord's suffering means in your own life? After a time of silent reflection, ask, "Would anyone like to share something meaningful about your pilgrimage?"
✧ **Receiving and celebrating God's grace**
Go around the circle, receiving and giving a word of grace.
✧ **Renewing discipleship**
  • Continue the wilderness journey of praying, reading the scripture and reading *Wilderness Wanderings* (chapter 6 for next week; chapter 7 is for Easter morning).
  • Continue to journal if it is meaningful to your pilgrimage.
  • Continue to take steps in the spiritual disciplines.
  • Write a letter of forgiveness. When you read "Hearing the Whispers" in chapter 6, think of a particular person whom

you need to or would like to forgive. Write a letter to that person, expressing your forgiveness in words.(You don't have to mail it.)

- Bring a candle, a holder, and something that has been espe-cially meaningful to you during this Lenten pilgrimage as we celebrate our last session together next week.

✧ **Returning to God's world**
Close with a prayer, sending the *Wanderers* forth into Holy Week with prayerful hearts.

(***Note to leader:*** *Select four readers for next week and have four copies of the same version of the Bible available for them. Next week's session includes an alternate plan that you can adapt for the group. If you use the alternate plan, you will need a tablecloth, a match, an unsliced loaf of bread, a pitcher of water, a large bowl with napkin or small towel to represent foot washing and servanthood, some extra candles and holders in case a Wanderer forgets, and a drinking glass for each person.*)

6. WANDERING IN THE SHADOW OF THE CROSS
(Holy Week)

The *Wanderers* have the usual time of reconnecting with one another. Then during the time of recentering in prayerful silence, the leader covers the table with a cloth, places an unsliced loaf of bread (previously broken in half) in the center of the table, sets the pitcher of water on one side and the bowl and napkin on the other. Arrange the *unlit* candles on the table in an attractive way.

Without comment, ask the selected readers to begin the reading:

(Preparation for Passover)	Matthew 26:17-19
	Mark 14:12-16
	Luke 22:7-13
(Washing disciples' feet)	John 13:1-20
(Jesus' awareness of betrayal)	Matthew 26:20-25
	Mark 14:17-21
	John 13:21-30

Moments of Silent Reflection

(New Commandment)	John 13:31-35

Moments of Silent Reflection and Silent Prayer

Leader

Amen. One of the four ancient symbols of the Christian Pascha, the Passion of Christ, is the Eucharist, the Lord's Supper. As we sit at table together, the bread in the center represents that sacrament. A second symbol is the Word. (*The leader places the*

Bible in front of the bread.) A third symbol is light. (*The leader says from memory a favorite verse of scripture—for example, "I am the light of the world"—and lights his or her candle with a match, then passes the candle to the person on the right.*)

Wanderers

(*Each person says from memory a favorite verse of scripture and lights a candle, then passes the leader's candle to the next person until everyone's candle is lit.*)

Leader

(*The leader passes the glasses around the table so that each person has one.*) The final ancient symbol is water. With water you were baptized, called to ministry—to servanthood—in the name of Jesus Christ. (*The leader pours water into the glass of the person to the right.*) Drink of the water that sustains you.

Wanderers

(*The person drinks of the water.*)

Leader

And pour out your life for others. (*The leader passes the pitcher to that same person.*)

Wanderers

(*Repeat this litany around the table, each person saying the words, drinking the water, and pouring water into the next person's glass.*)

Leader

I add to these ancient symbols, a symbol of my own wilderness wanderings through this Lenten season. (*The leader places on the table something that represents his or her own Lenten journey and explains its meaning.*)

Wanderers

(*Beginning with the person to the right, each person offers a symbol of the journey and explains it—unless a person chooses not to do so.*)

Leader

Let us join hands and pray silently in holy communion with God and one another. (*All remain silent until the leader feels the prayer is concluded.*) Amen. Go in silence. Our Lord is in his time of suffering.

All leave in silence.

GUIDE FOR A ONE-DAY LENTEN RETREAT

The Introduction suggests a format for reading the book. The WANDERERS IN COMMUNITY and A WORD FOR LEADERS found in the GUIDE FOR GROUP LENTEN PILGRIMAGE also apply to a retreat setting. Participants need to read the book *prior* to the retreat. Adapt the following outline based on the length of the retreat:

✧ **Recentering through silence and prayer**
See PRAYER in chapter 4 for different ways to pray.

✧ **Reading the scripture**
See SCRIPTURE in chapter 2 for different ways to read the scripture; also see the African model in the GUIDE FOR GROUP LENTEN PILGRIMAGE for the first week of Lent.

✧ **Thinking and reflecting**
Use the questions at the end of the chapter to guide discussion.

✧ **Recreating**
Offer time and freedom to relax, play, or pray together.
[Repeat the above steps as appropriate for the length of the retreat.]

✧ **Repenting**
Kathleen Norris in her book *Dakota* quotes a contemporary monk who suggests that repentance has to do with renouncing our narrow human views that are too small for God's mystery. Think about a time when something happened in the congregation or the denomination that triggered a negative feeling in you. If your feeling was intense, reflect on whether the source of your feeling could have been a view that is perhaps too narrow for God's mystery. Consider the "passions" that have hold of you. Silently unmask before God.

✧ **Receiving and celebrating God's grace**
Give one another and receive from one another a word of grace.

✧ **Renewing discipleship**
For ideas, see "Renewing discipleship" section in the GUIDE.

✧ **Returning to God's world with prayerful hearts**
Close with the closing celebration in the GUIDE for Holy Week or with the Eucharist if the retreat involves a clergy person.

NOTES

CHAPTER ONE: WANDERING IN THE WILDERNESS

1. From *Ashes to Fire* (Nashville: Abingdon, 1979), 19, 47.
2. Fred B. Craddock, et. al., *Preaching the New Common Lectionary, Year A* (Nashville: Abingdon Press, 1986), 12.
3. *The Sayings of the Desert Fathers: The Alphabetical Collection*, trans. Benedicta Ward, rev. ed. (Kalamazoo, Mich.: Cistercian Publications, 1984), 172.

CHAPTER TWO: WANDERERS CALLED BY CHRIST

1. Thomas Merton, *The Sign of Jonas* (New York: Harcourt. Brace, and Company, 1953), 268.
2. Quoted in *Western Asceticism* (Philadelphia: The Westminster Press, 1958), 197.
3. Boniface Ramsey, "The Spirituality of the Early Church: Patristic Sources," in *Spiritual Traditions*, 175.
4. Barbara Bedolla and Dominic Totaro, "Ignatian Spirituality," in *Spiritual Traditions*, 175.
5. Quoted in Henri J. M. Nouwen, *The Way of the Heart* (New York: First Ballantine Books, Epiphany Edition, 1983), 35.
6. Quoted in *The Sayings of the Desert Fathers*, 18.
7. Quoted in Mary Lou Kownacki, "Meetings on the Journey Can Break Heart Open," *National Catholic Reporter* 31, no. 18 (March 3, 1995): 2.
8. Nancy Roth, *The Breath of God: An Approach to Prayer* (Cambridge, MS: Cowley Publications, 1990), 136–37.
9. Quoted in *The Breath of God*, 137.

CHAPTER THREE: WANDERERS WITH HALOS AND CLAY FEET

1. Quoted in *Sayings of the Desert Fathers*, 6.
2. Howard A. Snyder, *EarthCurrents: The Struggle for the World's Soul* (Nashville: Abingdon Press, 1995), 79, quoting R. Monastersky, "Global Warming: Politics Muddle Policy," *Science News* 137, no. 25 (June 23, 1990): 391.
3. Nachman of Breslov, *The Empty Chair: Finding Hope and Joy: Timeless Wisdom from a Hasidic Master* (Woodstock, VT: Jewish Lights Publishing, 1994), 15.
4. Quoted in *Sayings of the Desert Fathers*, 2.

CHAPTER FOUR: WORDS FOR WANDERERS
1. Quoted in *Western Asceticism*, 143.
2. Quoted by Gwen White at Louisiana Conference United Methodist Women's Retreat, 1993.
3. Edwin H. Friedman at a seminar in Baton Rouge, Louisiana, sponsored by the Louisiana United Methodist Center for Pastoral Effectiveness, 1993.
4. Quoted in *Western Asceticism*, 99.
5. Psalm 22:1, 11, 14, 15, 16, 17, 18, 20.
6. Psalm 22:24, 26, 27, 29, 30-31.

CHAPTER FIVE: WITNESSING TO THE WONDER
1. Quoted in Taylor Branch, *Parting the Waters: America in the King Years 1954–63* (New York: Simon & Schuster, Inc., 1988), 45.
2. Joseph Campbell, *Myths to Live By* (New York: Bantam Books, 1973), 67.
3. For a simple, practical application of RET, see Jill Anderson, *Thinking, Changing, Rearranging: Improving Self-Esteem in Young People* (Eugene, OR: Timberline Press, 1981).
4. Jurgen Moltmann, *The Experiment of Hope* (London: SCM Press, 1975). Quoted in David J. Bosch, *Transforming Mission* (Maryknoll, New York: Orbis Books, 1991), 473.
5. Edwin C. Friedman in lecture at Ministers' Week, Perkins School of Theology, Dallas, Texas, Feb. 6, 1991.
6. Frederick Buechner, *The Sacred Journey* (New York: Harper & Row, 1982). Quoted in *Voices from the Heart: Four Centuries of American Piety* (Grand Rapids, MI: William B. Eerdmans Publishing Company, 1987), 112.

CHAPTER SIX: WANDERING IN THE SHADOW OF THE CROSS
1. Jack Finegan, *The Archeology of the New Testament: The Life of Jesus and the Beginning of the Early Church* (Princeton: Princeton University Press, 1969), 92. Other versions of John 11:18 place Bethany about "fifteen stadia" or "furlongs" from Jerusalem, which is the equivalent of about two miles.

BIBLIOGRAPHY

Anderson, James D., and Ezra Earl Jones. *Ministry of the Laity.* San Francisco: Harper & Row, Publishers, 1986.

Berry, Thomas. *The Dream of the Earth.* San Francisco: Sierra Club Books, 1988.

Bellah, Robert N. "Leadership Viewed from the Vantage Point of American Culture," *Origins* 20, no. 14 (September 13, 1990).

Bondi, Roberta. *To Love as God Loves: Conversations with the Early Church.* Philadelphia: Fortress Press, 1987.

———. *To Pray and to Love: Conversations on Prayer with the Early Church.* Minneapolis: Fortress Press, 1991.

Bonhoeffer, Dietrich. *Life Together.* New York: Harper & Brothers, Publishers, 1954.

Bosch, David J. *Transforming Mission: Paradigm Shifts in Theology of Mission.* Maryknoll, NY: Orbis Books, 1991.

Branch, Taylor. *Parting the Waters: America in the King Years 1954-63.* NY: Simon & Schuster Inc., 1989.

Buechner, Frederick. *The Sacred Journey.* San Francisco: Harper & Row, Publishers, 1982.

———. *Telling Secrets.* San Francisco: HarperSanFrancisco, 1991.

———. *Wishful Thinking: A Theological ABC.* New York: Harper & Row, Publishers, 1973.

Campbell, Joseph. *Myths to Live By.* New York: Bantam Books, 1972.

Christian Spirituality: The Essential Guide to the Most Influential Spiritual Writings of the Christian Tradition. Ed. Frank N. Magill and Ian P. McGreal. San Francisco: Harper & Row, Publishers, 1988.

Cobb, John B., Jr. *Lay Theology.* St. Louis: Chalice Press, 1994.

Craddock, Fred B. et al. *Preaching the New Common Lectionary, Year A.* Nashville: Abingdon Press, 1986.

Dillard, Annie. *Pilgrim at Tinker Creek.* New York: Harper & Row, Publishers, 1974.

Dodd, C. H. *Benefits of His Passion.* New York: Abingdon Press, 1956.

Doherty, Catherine de Heuck, *Poustinia: Christian Spirituality of the East for Western Man.* Notre Dame, IN: Ave Maria Press, 1974.

Fenhagen, James C. *Ministry and Solitude: Ministry of the Laity and the Clergy in Church and Society.* New York: Seabury Press, 1981.

Finegan, Jack. *The Archeology of the New Testament: The Life of Jesus and the Beginning of the Early Church*. Princeton: Princeton University Press, 1969.

Fiorenza, Elisabeth Schüssler, and Urban T. Holmes. *Proclamation 2: Lent: Series B*. Philadelphia: Fortress Press, 1981.

Foster, Richard J. *Celebration of Discipline: The Path to Spiritual Growth*. San Francisco: Harper & Row, Publishers, 1978.

Fox, Matthew. *Creation Spirituality: Liberating Gifts for the Peoples of the Earth*. San Francisco: HarperSanFrancisco, 1991.

Friedman, Edwin H. *Generation to Generation: Family Process in Church and Synagogue*. New York: The Guilford Press, 1985.

From Ashes to Fire. Nashville: Abingdon, 1979.

Gealy, Fred D. *Celebration*. Nashville: Graded Press, 1969.

Gutiérrez, Gustavo. *We Drink from Our Own Wells: The Spiritual Journey of a People*. Trans. Matthew J. O'Connell. Maryknoll, NY: Orbis Books, 1984.

Hall, Thelma. *Too Deep for Words: Rediscovering Lectio Divina*. New York: Paulist Press, 1988.

Harper's Bible Commentary. Ed. James L. Mays. San Francisco: Harper & Row, Publishers, 1988.

Harper's Bible Dictionary. Ed. Paul J. Achtemeier. San Francisco: Harper & Row, Publishers, 1985.

"Harper's Index, *Harper's Magazine* (January 1995).

Howe, Reuel. *Herein Is Love*. Valley Forge: The Judson Press, 1961.

Job, Rueben. *A Guide to Retreat for All God's Shepherds*. Nashville: Abingdon Press, 1994.

Jones, Alan W. *Soul Making: The Desert Way of Spirituality*. San Francisco: Harper & Row, Publishers, 1985.

Kelsey, Morton T. *The Other Side of Silence: A Guide to Christian Meditation*. New York: Paulist Press, 1976.

Kingsbury, Jack Dean, and Chester Pennington. *Proclamation 2: Lent: Series A*. Philadelphia: Fortress Press, 1980.

Lawrence, Brother, of the Resurrection. *The Practice of the Presence of God*. Trans. John J. Delaney. New York: Doubleday Image Books, 1977.

The Lives of the Desert Fathers: The Historia Monachorum in Aegypto. Trans. Norman Russell. London: A. R. Mowbray and Co. Ltd., 1981.

The Lord of the Journey: A Reader in Christian Spirituality. Ed. Roger Pooley and Philip Seddon. London: Collins, 1986.

Madden, Myron C. *The Power to Bless*. Nashville: Broadman Press, 1970.

Meehan, Brenda. *Holy Women of Russia: The Lives of Five Orthodox Women Offer Spiritual Guidance for Today.* San Francisco: HarperSanFrancisco, 1993.

✓Merton, Thomas. *The Sign of Jonas.* New York: Harcourt, Brace and Company, 1953.

Micks, Marianne H., and Thomas E. Ridenhour. *Proclamation 2: Lent: Series C.* Philadelphia: Fortress Press, 1979.

Nachman of Breslov. *The Empty Chair: Finding Hope and Joy: Timeless Wisdom from a Hasidic Master.* Woodstock, VT: Jewish Lights Publishing, 1994.

✓Norris, Kathleen. *Dakota: A Spiritual Geography.* New York: Ticknor & Fields, 1993.

✓Nouwen, Henri J.M. "An Invitation to the Spiritual Life," *Leadership* (Summer 1981).

——. *Here and Now: Living in the Spirit.* New York: Crossroad Publishing Company, 1994.

——. *Life of the Beloved: Spiritual Living in a Secular World.* New York: Crossroad, 1992.

——. "Spiritual Direction," *Reflections* (Jan. 1981).

——. *The Way of the Heart.* New York: Ballantine Books, 1983.

Oden, Thomas C. *Two Worlds: Notes on the Death of Modernity in America and Russia.* Downers Grove, IL: InterVarsity Press, 1992.

Oden, William B. *Liturgy as Life-Journey.* Los Angeles: Acton House, Inc., Publishers, 1976.

Palmer, Parker. "Action and Insight: An Interview with Parker Palmer," *The Christian Century* (March 22–29, 1995), 326–29.

Pelikan, Jaroslav. *The Melody of Theology: A Philosophical Dictionary.* Cambridge, MA: Harvard University Press, 1988.

Roth, Nancy. *The Breath of God: An Approach to Prayer.* Cambridge MA: Cowley Publications, 1990.

The Sayings of the Desert Fathers: The Alphabetical Collection. Rev. ed. Trans. Benedicta Ward. Kalamazoo, MI: Cistercian Publications, 1984.

Snyder, Howard A. *EarthCurrents: The Struggle for the World's Soul.* Nashville: Abingdon Press, 1995.

Soards, Marion L., Thomas Dozeman, and Kendall McCabe. *Preaching the Revised Common Lectionary.* Nashville: Abingdon Press, 1994.

Spiritual Traditions for the Contemporary Church. Ed. Robin Maas and Gabriel O'Donnell. Nashville: Abingdon Press, 1990.

Steindl-Rast, David. *Gratefulness, the Heart of Prayer: An Approach to Life in Fullness.* New York: Paulist Press, 1984.

The Study of Spirituality. Eds. Cheslyn Jones, Geoffrey Wainwright, and Edward Yarnold. New York: Oxford University Press, 1986.

Stuempfle, Herman G., Jr., and Peter J. Kearney. *Proclamation: Lent: Series C*. Philadelphia: Fortress Press, 1973.

Toelken, Barre. "Seeing with a Native Eye: How Many Sheep Will It Hold?" *Seeing with a Native Eye: Essays on Native American Religion*. Ed. Walter H. Caps. New York: Harper & Row, Publishers, 1976.

Tournier, Paul. *The Meaning of Persons*. New York: Harper & Row, Publishers, 1957.

Underhill, Evelyn. *Practical Mysticism*. New York: E. P. Dutton, 1943.

Voices from the Heart: Four Centuries of American Piety. Ed. Roger Lundin and Mark A. Noll. Grand Rapids, MI: William B. Eerdmans Publishing Company, 1987.

Wall, James M. "A Show in Which Prayer Is All in the Family," *The Christian Century* (May 15–22, 1991), 539–40.

Wallis, Jim. *The Call to Conversion: Recovering the Gospel for These Times*. San Francisco: Harper & Row, Publishers, 1981.

The Way of a Pilgrim and *The Pilgrim Continues His Way*. Trans. R. M. French. New York: Seabury Press, 1965.

Weems, Lovett H. *Leadership*, Saint Paul School of Theology (Sept. 1990).

Western Asceticism. Ed. Owen Chadwick. Philadelphia: The Westminster Press, 1958.

The Westminster Dictionary of Christian Spirituality. Ed. Gordon S. Wakefield. Philadelphia: Westminster Press, 1983.

The Westminster Dictionary of Worship. Ed. J. G. Davies. Philadelphia: The Westminster Press, 1972.

White, James F. *Sacraments as God's Self Giving*. Nashville: Abingdon Press, 1983.

Wilkes, Paul. "The Hands That Would Shape Our Souls," *The Atlantic* (Dec. 1990).

To the Church in Spain, we have converted the natives — they are now prepared for slavery. (handwritten)

About the Author

MARILYN BROWN ODEN is the author of five previous books and is a seminar and retreat leader. A United Methodist laywoman, she has traveled extensively, participating in congregations and mission work globally, including Russia and Bosnia. In 1992, she received the Distinguished Achievement Award from Dillard University in New Orleans, and she serves on the Board of Trustees of Saint Paul School of Theology in Kansas City. With double master's degrees in counseling and creative writing, she has been a teacher, counselor, and adjunct professor of writing. Her two most recent books are *365 Meditations for Grandmothers* and *Land of Sickles and Crosses*. She is married to Bishop William B. Oden.